If the way that you've always done things works perfectly and achieves the outcomes you desire then great - keep going, as the results you are likely to get in the future will be broadly the same.

If not, then change! Learn new ways, challenge everything and think!

if you always do what you've always done you'll always get what you've always got

First Published 2002 by
Capstone Publishing Limited (A Wiley Company)
8 Newtec Place
Magdalen Road
Oxford
OX4 1RE
United Kingdom
http://www.capstoneideas.com

Library of Congress Cataloging-in-Publication Data

A CIP catalogue record for this book is available from the
British Library

ISBN 1- 84112- 4370

Typeset in Eureka Sans
Printed and bound Singapore by Imago Publishing Limited

Substantial discounts on bulk quantities of Capstone Books
are available to corporations, professional associations and
other organisations. For details telephone Capstone Publishing
on (+44-1865-798623), fax (+44-1865-240941) or email
(info@wiley-capstone.co.uk)

DEDICATION

To James and James and Sara and Gareth

Always think!

think!

by Tina Catling and Mark Davies

CAPSTONE

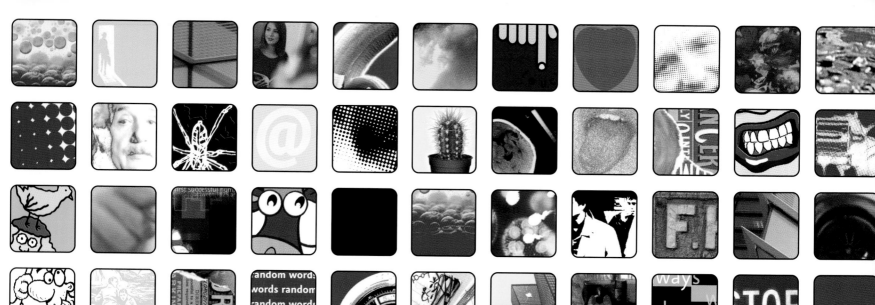

c○ntents

Chapter 1. Challenge This is a wake up call to all those with a lazy mind, to inspire imagination and challenge existing ways of thinking. 11

Chapter 2. Stimulus What is it that you could use to add that extra spark and unlock your potential? 31

Chapter 3. Techniques Effective thinking is a skill which can be improved by using the right techniques. 41

Chapter 4. Interesting People What do the experts from business, the arts and science say? Learn the secrets of their success or just be inspired. 71

Chapter 5. Case Studies Some examples of how improving your thought process can have amazing results. 93

Chapter 6. Mental Mental gymnastics to push you through comfort zones and stretch your imagination. 103

Chapter 7. Physical Our thinking is affected by our physical state. Explore ways to stimulate and improve thought through physical senses. 123

Chapter 8. Oh really! Yes... oh really! Some surprising stimulations. 142

Wealth warning!

Having the ability to

think professionally is a

very powerful asset.

You may create

hundreds of profitable

ideas and earn

a fortune.

Think! is like the grit that creates the pearl. A unique collection of pages to amuse, inspire and educate, but most of all to stimulate the 'spark' that will lead to your next incredible idea. We hope that every time you need to think you will grab this resource and flick through the pages. Just let the images pass by your eyes and fuel your mind or read the words and go a little deeper... or do both simultaneously.

Thinking is as natural as breathing and walking. So natural that we take it for granted. Most of us do not actively think about how we think or how our thinking could be improved or the effect that it could have at work or at home.

Just think about it!

Professional thinkers, active thinkers, examine the process and consider how to enhance their skills. They experiment, they play, they don't mind if they say something new out loud.

We know that visual stimuli, a change of environment, colours, images, music and food can all enhance our thinking processes. As professional, creative thinkers, when the *outside the box* team need ideas they grab a pile of magazines, photo library books, toys, music tapes, food and pile into the garden or wherever they think would be stimulating to discuss ideas and they actually 'think!'

Sitting in a meeting with others or sitting alone in a bland room and trying to conceive of new thoughts and ideas without any visual stimulation is very constraining. **New ideas thrive in an environment that is positive, colourful, pictorial; even musical, beautiful and sensual**. It helps your mind to be set free if you feel surrounded with intriguing images, sounds, smells and tastes. When all your senses are alert and you feel relaxed it is easier to become more open minded and creative.

With the world moving as fast as it does it is not just important but vital that we all know how to think in a creative and innovative way - corporately and in our everyday lives. **But if creativity is a survival skill then where is the manual?**

Inside this book is an exciting and stimulating mix of colours, images, stories of how others get creative, poetry, art with notes on how the artist was inspired.

There are pictures of the animal world with intriguing questions like how would bees solve your problem?

You'll also find selected creativity techniques - from some of the best minds around - and quotes from great leaders.

This guide is something to cherish and enjoy - just like creativity. It could be used on your own or as a tool in a team meeting.

We noticed that some people find creative thinking difficult and do not have the same resources to hand as our teams do, so the idea of *Think!* was born - a book which would inspire imagination, encourage creativity, challenge existing ways of thinking, unlock potential and enhance creative thinking skills.

We researched hundreds of books about creative thinking techniques. The techniques and concepts in many of them are excellent and the theories often well researched but, at that critical moment when it counts and you are sitting staring at a white sheet of paper, these books may not help. We couldn't find what we were looking for, so we created it ourselves. But why bother being more creative and thinking about how you think?

Well ...
You will have more and better ideas!
You will increase your personal productivity!
You will stay ahead of your competitors!
You will feel more stimulated!
You will have more fun!

think!

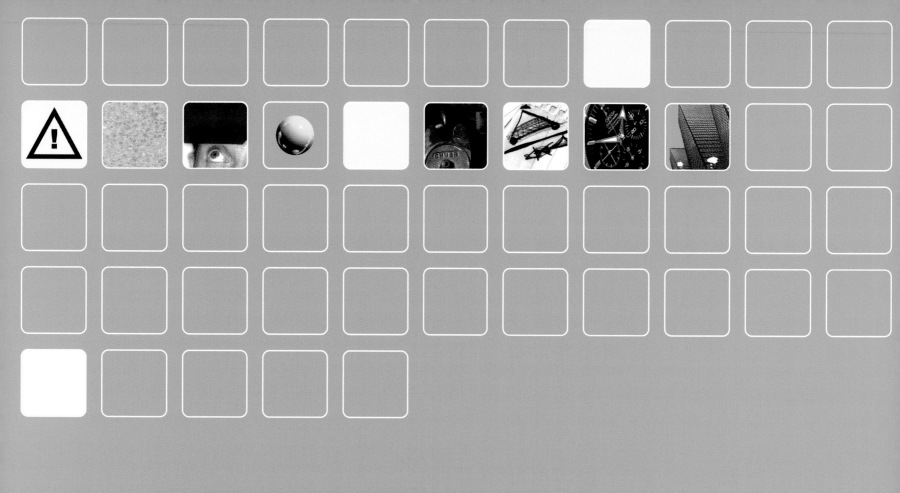

Challenge

Have you ever wondered if you've let your thinking get a little lazy? Do you ever really think about how you think?

This section should act as a wet fish slapped in your face - wake up your mind, shake it up, play with new ways of thinking. It's your challenge.

dangerous assumptions ahead

Novel, creative, stimulating thought often involves taking the risk of breaking away from your normal comfortable patterns of thinking about things or doing things.

Consider the things that have always been done in a certain way in your organisation - the systems and procedures, the product, design and the service and delivery... We call these set ways of doing things the "normalies" - for example: "Oh we 'normally' do the billing at the end of every month" or "We 'normally' call our clients once every quarter." Have these 'normalies' developed because they are the best and most effective solutions or because it has always been done like that and nobody has ever challenged the status quo?

We all make assumptions about certain things and one of the most dangerous assumptions we make is to believe that the systems, procedures, structures, products and services we work with every day are good enough just because they are already there. But good enough should never be enough.

To create it is important to challenge - ask "Why do we do it this way?" Then ask "Is there a better way?" - "How could we improve?" Don't wait for someone to ask you to review - ask the challenging questions now.

You don't need to cause a revolution. You can just make a few little changes that will improve things, but at least you are challenging and thinking.

When *was* the last time you sat down and really thought about your systems, services, procedures and your products?

Don't just do - Think!

We heard about someone who was always in the gym - pumping iron and running and sweating - but they never seemed to change shape. The effort and time expended was completely disproportionate to the result. We later learned that it is critical when doing exercise to do it in an effective manner - a personal trainer told us that he sees people every day wasting time and energy exercising ineffectively - "they could be twice as effective in half the time if they did the exercises properly".

Sometimes we would be better to just stop for a moment and think about what we are doing and how effectively we are doing it, rather than continuing with the dangerous assumption that because we normally do it that way then that way is the best. **Don't have a lazy mind.**

Challenge all the "normalies" in your life and work and check they are there for all the best reasons.

Everyone learns differently. How do you learn? Some people learn best through sound - listening to the radio or a lecture. Some people are visual learners and prefer text and images and some of us need to experience something, to feel it to help us learn. The important thing is to think about how you can enjoy learning and do it often.

learn!

Live as if every day were your last. Learn as if you are going to live forever.

You've heard about lifelong learning, but what do you actively do to keep adding new information to your brain? Your brain is a bit like the Internet with millions of subjects you can search. But it can only search from the data that it holds. For example, if you were to use your brains search engine to find all the data it has on 'the ocean' - you'd immediately source vast amounts of knowledge on the subject. It is incredible what's in there!!

Good News!

Learning doesn't have to be from books and courses. You are absorbing information all the time through all of your senses, which is great because it means that learning can be fun - and it should be.

Learn with a passion

Actively think about all the sources of learning you have available to you immediately.

For example, people - when you meet someone new find out what they do: everything about their work and how they do it. When was the last time you did that?

Angora Jumpers!

Where does the Angora come from? What is it? How does it become a jumper?

We have a friend in Northern Ireland called Sara Templeton. She worked on a Kibbutz for a year in Israel and one of her jobs was to shave the Angora Rabbits! When you meet an Angora Rabbit Shaver it's fascinating to find out everything about their work...

The more knowledge and information you can get into your head the more chance you have of creating new ideas. As Sir Tom Farmer says "nothing comes from nothing" and you never know when knowing all about shaving rabbits will come in handy!

When your own personal search engine is looking for data in your head it will have a better chance if there is a wide variety of material to select from.

Jump out of your rut.

Explore!

Radio:	Listen to Radio 4 and then Radio 1
TV:	Watch wildlife programmes and black-and-white films
Books:	Read an academic book
Comics:	Read a comic
Pubs:	Ask someone in your local pub all about their work
Walks:	Stop when you are next out for a walk and examine the leaves on a tree
Offices:	What type of wood is your table made of and where is that from?
Shoes:	The leather for your shoes: how did it get that colour?
Trees:	Why do trees have bark?
Birds:	What do you know about the migration of swallows?
Gambling:	What is spread betting?
People Watching:	When was the last time you sat on a park bench and just watched everything?
Boats:	When was the last time you were in a boat?
Culture:	Go to the theatre and the opera and the ballet
Sport:	Go to see a sport live that you have never seen before
Magazines:	Read a Science magazine, a Women's magazine and a lads' magazine

Consider the diversity of knowledge that is out there just waiting for you to go and enjoy it - that's lifelong learning and it's fun!

Go on gorge yourself, fill your brain up - really stuff it full! (And there's no calories in knowledge either!)

BREAK OUT

BREAK OUT

We often restrain ourselves from being as creative as we can. We hold ourselves in a mental straight jacket.

We don't want to suggest anything foolish. We know we are not creative - we've been told that before. Creative people are those who are wild and wacky - aren't they?

Wrong!

You must release yourself from these thoughts as they will hold you back. The fact is that whether you think you can, or you think you can't, you are right.

Experiment - explore your own unique creativity. This evening why not try something new, paint a picture, write a story, sing a song.

Blow the cobwebs out of your mind and let some fresh creative air in now!

Do you ever complain that you don't have enough time? You certainly don't have enough time to think! You're too busy with all that *doing* to be *thinking*. But there are literally hundreds of hours you have that you could liberate for your

thinking.

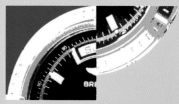

Research into company directors has shown that only 11% have their best ideas at work. 12% have them in the bath, 18% while in bed and 39% do their creative thinking when travelling.

When could you think?

So how much travelling or rather creative thinking time do you have?

Your travelling time could become your creative thinking time. Think! If you commute to work every day, between the ages of 22 and 65, taking one hour each way, then you will have spent 2.5 years in transit. **How many ideas could you conjure up if you could just sit about thinking for two and a half years?**

time

liberate
some
thinking
time

| 5 | 4 | 3 | 2 | 1 | before it's too late

how many ideas could you conjure
up if you could just sit about
thinking for two and a half years?

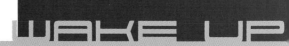

Join up the nine dots with four straight lines without taking your pencil off the paper.

HINT Be careful not to make any assumptions about the instructions - think outside the box.

If you can't rise to the challenge, you'll find the solution at www.outsidethebox.co.uk

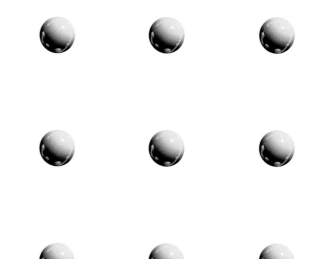

PLAY MIND GAMES

It's very strange that even though your brain has no moving parts you feel something working when you think. Try it.

Brazilian frog green

How many ways can you divide a square into four symmetrical parts? Try to achieve 10.

1   2   3   4   5

6   7   8   9   10

Play a game of word association with a subject that you need to think more creatively about. Start with a simple word, **'out'** for example - if you need to think of ways you might motivate a team start with '**motivation**' (then move on), forward, path, walk, run, car, journey, adventure, novelty...

Keep going with this and then use the words to help to spark some new ideas to motivate your team. With the example above, you might think of putting a path down one of your corridors which shows how far the team have got towards their aim.

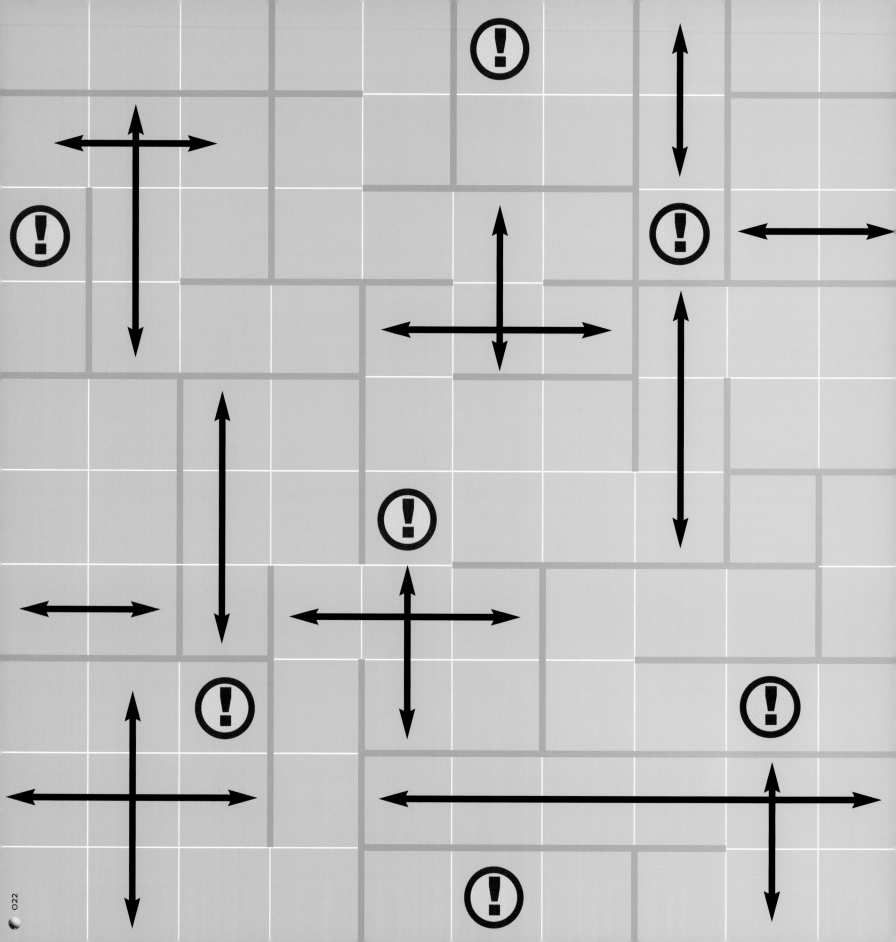

Do you get lost in thought because you don't go there often or because you need a map?

It is important to make yourself think in different ways so that new ideas can flourish. Try drawing a picture that represents you. Was that so difficult?

If it was, it's probably because you haven't thought of doing it for quite some time.

"It's silly and irrelevant."
Wrong!

Liberate yourself - allow yourself to express your thoughts in new and creative ways.

Do you ever get lost in thought?

  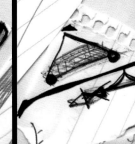

"Life is either a daring adventure
or nothing at all"

Helen Keller

how far can you go?

If you find that you always think about
the same things in the same way perhaps
you need to expand your experiences.

If you keep on learning from new experiences
you will increase your store of material from
which you can draw ideas.

When was the last time you really felt a
stretch - you know, when you felt excited
and a little scared about trying
something new?

What would scare you a little?

A presentation to the board?
To lead a brainstorm? To jump from a plane?

Do you know where your comfort zone is?
How comfortable are you doing what you do?

Go on... stretch!

STOP
(and think!)

Do you know where your comfort zone is?
How comfortable are you doing what you do?

025

It isn't your company that creates all the ideas and innovations, it is the people in it who do. You do. Remember that when you next have to create some new thinking. You may feel daunted by the task but your company cannot create unique ideas without you - in fact **nobody in the world creates ideas exactly like you do.** Allow yourself some time to use the ideas in this book and think, explore different techniques or just let your mind wander... the ideas will come.

Allow yourself to be brave enough to think unique, individual thoughts and then have the courage to share them with colleagues.

Being creative at work takes some courage. You want to be sure you don't say anything out of place or silly. You know that you need to create some new ideas to move things forward, but... there are a million excuses.

GET OFF YOUR "BUT"! It's too easy to say... "I would be creative - but"

Would you say that your company culture supports creativity? Is there time to think? Are the people you work with supportive and encouraging and non-judgmental? Do you celebrate success? Do you learn from failures in a positive way?

If you answered 'no' to any of these then WHY NOT CHANGE THINGS?

It is important to get up and do something about the environment in which you work - ask questions, start behaving in an encouraging and supportive way with your team. Hold a meeting today to ask for ways that things could be improved so it makes everyone feel more creative.

Behaviour breeds behaviour and it starts with you.

Be positive and generous - really listen to the ideas of others and help them to put their ideas into action, then they will listen to your ideas and support you.

Don't sit back and wait for someone else to fix things - do it yourself!

Allow yourself to be brave enough to think unique, individual thoughts and then have the courage to share them with colleagues.

companies aren't creative individuals are

Take a word and let your mind flow - this is stream of conciousness. Read each word and consider how it links to the next - this is great mental exercise. Try your own word flow and see if it leads you to any novel ideas.

control parental mummy egypt pyramid build team captain navigation oceanography travel propeller aeroplane mahogany woodwind mistral surf saltwater halibut chips board director movies blue peter pan cook beef argument reconcile arbitrate union jack rustle leaves book school educate experiment beagles hunt gather harvest combine twosome intimate knowledge develop nurture newborn foal jockey club working effort commitment court criminal innocent youth potential future hope despair war murder detect metal precious children play act freeze fridge football passion lust money riches poverty trap mouse mat wipe out roller flash light dark secret covert operation surgeon blood type key enter world new old pension post fence lunge train passenger embark journey experience raw hard strive stars planets hollywood film animate exaggerate promise contract illness terminal airport fly sky crash course drive speed email first class room build city limit over weight gain lose out in vogue magazine women femininity fragrance orchid white wine cask ale pub laughter joy news disaster die rebirth evolve adapt change notes communicate media format proportion architecture renaissance movement energy art creation eden vegetation jungle tarzan ape fool jester joker cards stud stallion pedigree mongrel fifty seven variety spice orient asia east wing bird egg head brain wave tide high low point shoot target weapon war tank aquatic fish reef joint beef discuss debate heat foreign desert drought africa victim aid first win always forever infinite wisdom intelligent life longevity stamina pace maker my lord manor cockney arthur king england patriot games olympic greece ancient ruin drink feck ted bear zoo animal instinct natural colour tone body physique macho strut stuff taxidermy preserve jam traffic volume waveband radio dj feature character inherant family values moral maze lost found search light heavy weight paper chase girls charm chat libido frustration release free offer interest account add extend trot dressage fetlock muscle power **control**

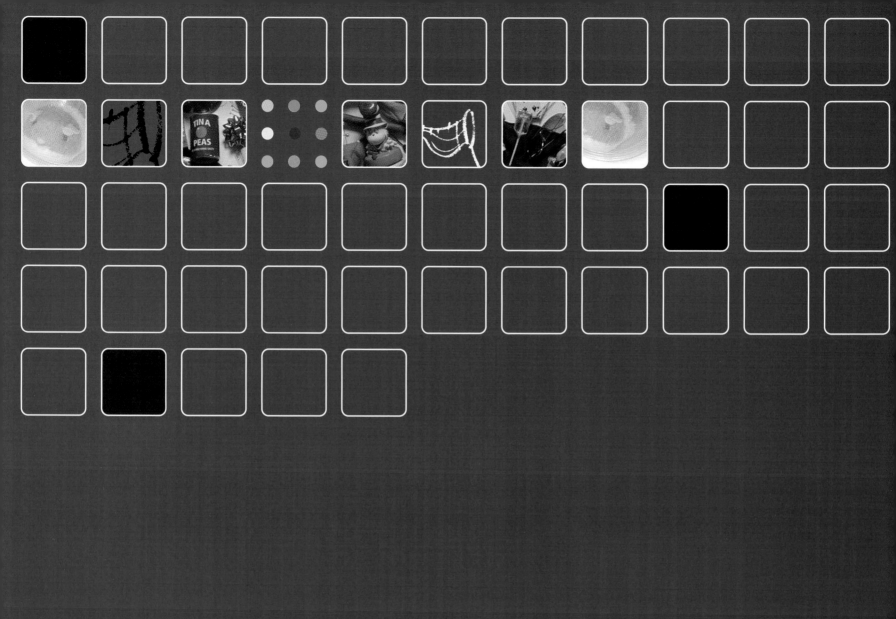

Stimulus

We all need stimulus to help us think. This is the very reason for this book. As Sir Tom Farmer says – "nothing comes from nothing".

In this section we offer some ideas on how you can jump-start your creative thinking by using words, teams, colours, architecture, junk, even sins .....

Different colours make you feel different emotions. Different emotions affect how your thinking works. Consider what colours would be useful for you to create ideas for your specific need. Do you need a bold, radical, strong solution or a soft, subtle one? Seeing red? Or feeling blue? Lost your colour? Or green with envy? Tickled pink?

colour
your emotions

It's fascinating when you think about how we use the language of colour every day and yet, when we discuss its importance to our mood we shun the idea as silly nonsense and certainly not a proper topic for business to be dwelling on! The colours around us fundamentally affect our moods and our moods affect how we think. It is important to understand the effects of different colours so that next time you want to think in a particular way you can go and find a space with that colour, or surround yourself with objects that will fill your space with that colour - or wear it!

Try wearing bright orange or red if you are feeling that you are lacking energy - try cream and brown if you want to feel softer and show more empathy.

Turquoise and bright, sunny yellow help stimulate positive and uplifting feelings and help us to be creative.

(Magnolia very rarely helps anyone to be creative!)

Red:
Red can escalate your energy levels and metabolism. An exciting, vibrant and passionate colour. Do you need more energy and pizzazz in your thinking? Try looking at red - wear a red tie or a red jacket.

Yellow:
Yellow is optimistic and uplifting. Do you need some humour for your thought processes? Yellow can cheer you up if you are feeling blue!

Blue:
Blue counters yellow - it calms. If you are stressed and can't think, try looking at blue. Blue sky, blue walls - cool, calm blue will help to remove some of the stress.

White:
White conveys sterility and innocence - a natural white can help you to make things seem less cluttered. If your thinking feels all jumbled up in your head, then head for a white space with no distractions.

Green:
Do you need fresh, lush ideas? Green is a peaceful natural colour - a colour that can inspire thoughts of the natural world.

Experiment with colour for yourself and see how it affects your thinking. What colour are the walls in the spaces where you often go to think?

by the way - magnolia very rarely helps anyone to be creative!!

Isn't it amazing how nearly all buildings

are different? That's literally hundreds of

thousands of ideas - different ways of solving

similar problems. New ideas for

- aesthetics

- materials

- surfaces.

Does an architect use all the senses to design a new building?

Think about architecture next time you are out - really look and think.

Consider what problems the architect had to overcome to build in that particular environment - how were these problems overcome?

What style was chosen? Why?

What materials were used? Why?

Letting your mind explore the issues in a new area exercises your thinking and stimulates thoughts for the issues you may be working on.

one man's rubbish

rubbish

The more intriguing the more likely that

Like magpies, our creative team at *outside the box* collect objects in a box near their desks. When they have to think of new ideas the box is a good place to start. Often objects, like images or words, can spark an idea.

A pen

A walking stick

A voodoo doll

A rubber chicken

A monkey

A false leg

A straw hat

A bottle of beer

A rubber stamp

A pot duck

A straw hat

A sponge football

A toy car

A cocktail shaker

What would you collect in your box of thinking things?

Looking through a treasure trove such as this you could get new ideas, for example if you had to create a new direction for marketing an insurance policy...

You might see the teddy and think Comfort - how comforting it is to have good insurance. Child - does the product protect the family? Bear - strong and protecting.

You might see a rock and think Solid - the policy will stand the test of time.

bits and pieces you collect you will have the stimulus for new thinking.

The seven deadly sins are often considered when searching for motivations to persuade people to purchase.

Use them as a quick thinking tool.

Can you think of how your product or service is sold and relate it to a sin?

Just quickly note them down as these examples show.

Sloth Makes life easy, earn more - do less

Greed Make more profits, increase your earning potential

Envy Imagine what the neighbours will say when they see your new car outside

Gluttony Go on - eat as much as you like - it's low fat

Pride You can put your certificate on your wall when you achieve a pass grade

Lust Aftershave that will have you running for cover

Vanity You will be so beautiful in this

Try to think of selling your product or service using these and then try to sell it without using them.

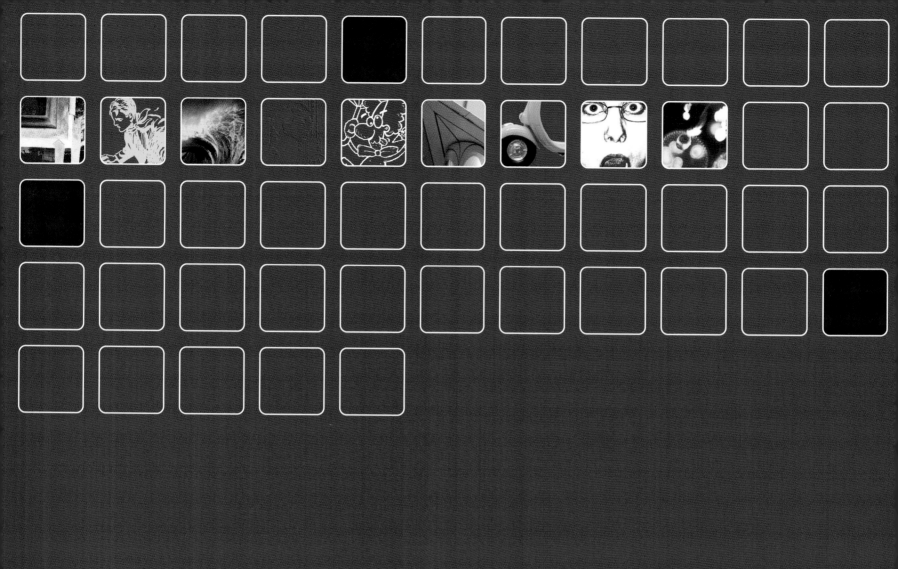

Techniques

There are numerous techniques you can try to help stimulate creative thinking. Some techniques are good for analysing where you are now and others for creating new ideas for the future. Some are good for creating many ideas and yet others for refining the pool of new thoughts down to a manageable few.

The more techniques you try the more likely you are to increase your thinking skills.

THINK

Be an avid observer

Do you use your body language to create rapport? Have you ever noticed that sometimes you just click with someone? When this happens you will find that you are probably mirroring their body posture and movements. Watch couples in a bar (but don't let them catch you!) - if they are in rapport they will be mirroring each other. You can consciously create rapport with this technique, and it helps the person you are working with to relax and enjoy creating new ideas with you more.

Think! Who buys your product or service now?

Who could buy your product or service if you just let them know about it?

Perhaps you could just adapt your product or service and they'd love it.

Think about all the people you would observe just walking down a busy street at lunchtime.

In fact don't just think about it - go out today and walk down a busy high street.

Who do you see? What are people wearing? How old are they? What colour are they? What size are they?

It is amazing to really notice the rich diversity on the high street!

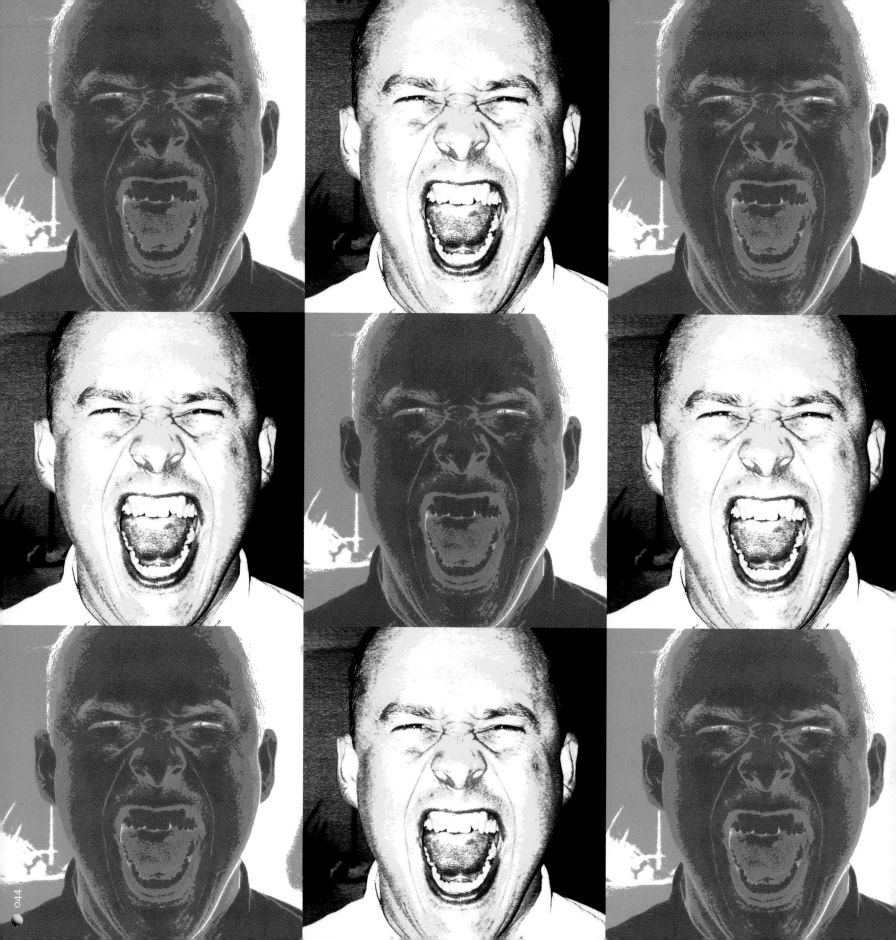

Why aren't we more creative?

We all get boxed in by certain restrictions and we need to understand these. First, can you recognise any of the boxes that your thinking gets trapped by?

Do you push your ideas away until they are dead?

1 I don't have the time
"I'm too busy to 'waste time' thinking"

2 I don't want to take a risk
"I can't take risks, it may go wrong"

What boxes trap your thinking?

7 There's only one way
"When I know the answer I don't waste time looking further"

8 I don't create waves
"Creative people can create problems and I like to keep things on an even keel"

3 I need it to be perfect
"I wouldn't want to be seen making mistakes"

4 I can only think answers are right/wrong - black/white
"I need clarity"

5 I'm not creative
"I've never been seen as a creative person, so I believe I am not"

6 I always think profits / profits
"I can't waste money on new, untested ideas"

Get over the hurdles
- think beyond the boundaries
you have created for yourself.

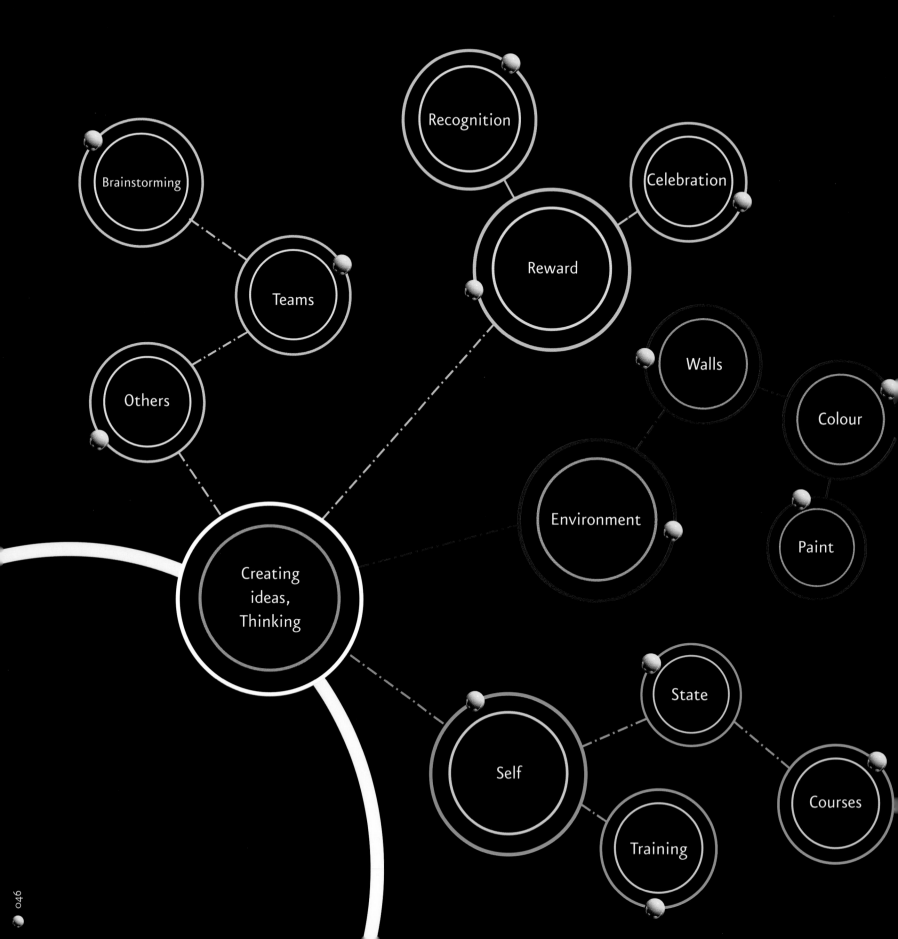

Recognition

Brainstorming

Celebration

Teams

Reward

Others

Walls

Colour

Environment

Creating
ideas,
Thinking

Paint

State

Self

Courses

Training

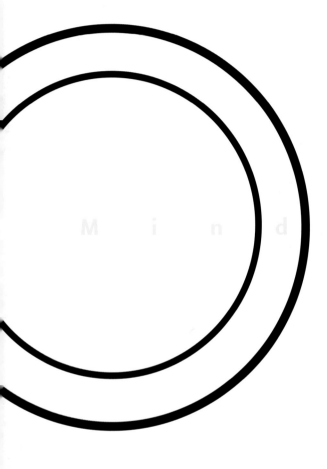

M a p p i n g

Originally developed by Tony Buzan, mind mapping works with the natural way your brain functions. Ideas spark in chains, not in rows or columns, by working out on tendrils from the core idea. Mind mapping can be done alone or with any number of people. If you create a mind map of your own it is useful to share it with others who can add to it. The rules for mind mapping are similar to those of brainstorming in that you need to allow ideas to flow freely. Initially don't restrain your thinking by judging your ideas; just write anything and everything down. You can edit your mind map later.

First, get the biggest piece of paper you can - flip chart paper is good - and you'll need some coloured pens. Begin by putting the original subject at the centre and then draw lines from that for the key areas. Then you simply keep adding and adding as ideas spark. You will find that some ideas then link up or double up and this is all part of the process. Often using colours for each of the main strands can help and using images - simple illustrations - can aid the process too.

Mind mapping helps you to create numerous insights as you think around the whole issue. Linear thinking can tend to lead you down only one line of thought, whereas mind mapping is marvellously expansive.

You may find mind mapping a little odd at first, or you may find it very easy immediately. The point is to try it a few times and try to let your mind flow.

Re

can't relate to the audience that you have to come up with ideas for, perhaps they may be 60+ or 4 to 5 year olds, then go into their world.

late?

Go on an adventure into other peoples' worlds. Go where they would go, talk to them, read what they would read, watch what they would watch, eat what they would eat. Note down your thoughts and feelings. Gather as many visual references of them as you can from magazines, etc., and simply have fun cutting out type, pictures, advertisements - anything relating to their world - and stick all these images on one or two boards. Now, you can use these 'mood' boards to capture some of the essence of who the people you need to create ideas for are - just look at the board or boards and think about their lives.

Then, when you think of ideas for them, ask "would they like it? would it fit? would it be relevant?" refer to your notes, experience and 'mood' boards and they will help.

Once upon a time...

Storytelling - now that is definitely not for business!

wrong!

Storytelling and metaphor are perfect ways to get new ideas.

Think about the area you need some fresh ideas for and tell the story about how the problem or issue began, what will be happening next and what the happy ending will be.

Take 30 minutes and write the story down: "Once upon a time, there was a company who never had any ideas... Then one day..."

Using a metaphor can help you see something in a completely new way. We were discussing the issues of customer relationship management recently, and it helped everyone to think of CRM as glue. Like the glue that sticks the customers to us - 'CRM Gum'! Complexity is often rendered to simplicity when someone suggests a metaphor - "Oh, so it's like..."

the end...
(or the beginning?)

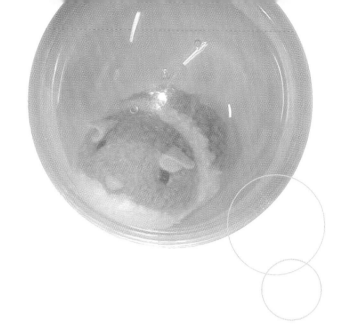

Gerbil

You have to use your imagination for this one!

It is useful to think about how your product or service is seen by others. Do you need a fresh perspective? Do you ever think about how animals would think about things?

If you were a gerbil you would look at things from a very new perspective! You'd be small and vulnerable. You would have to look up at things - how does your product & service look from the floor - from the ground up?

This idea could lead you to consider all the minute details or to think about any smaller or more vulnerable areas you need to focus on.

What about a bear's perspective - strong, brave, hairy? Perhaps this would lead you to consider being more assertive in your market - to stand on your own feet and growl - or to be brave about a new product launch. Not sure about the hair!

Thinking about different animals and their many characteristics can help to give new perspectives on your thinking.

Bird, Chameleon, Zebra, Dog, Peacock, Fish, Lion, Beaver, Frog, Shark, Snake, Cat, Turkey, Armadillo, Lesser spotted...

Grab them

Many of the great minds throughout our history have displayed their 'whole brain' thinking through their note taking. They use pictures, diagrams and notes - how do you capture your thoughts?

before they leave!

Post them on the wall, put them in a scrap book, use a note book or a Personal Digital Assistant, draw a mind map, use a dictaphone, pin them on a notice board, put them in a shoe box.

However you keep them, and it doesn't matter how, try to capture your thoughts and ideas as they pass - however bizarre and random they may seem. You never know when your ideas may come in handy.

As you start to build up your unique collection of thoughts you must try to organise or structure them so they become easier to use.

What categories would you choose?

When you start to organise the capturing of thoughts you will be surprised to find that it gains momentum. Tell people around you what you are doing and you will soon find that they too collect ideas to help you. Then share your thoughts with others and let them develop more ideas with you.

Your ideas are a valuable resource - keep them safe!

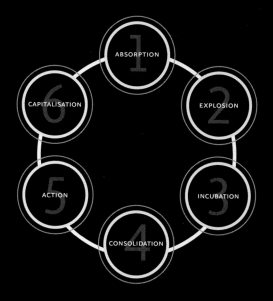

Process works (sometimes)

THIS MODEL CAN HELP YOU. EACH STAGE MUST BE FULLY COMPLETED
BEFORE THE NEXT IS BEGUN. FOLLOWED METHODICALLY THIS PROCESS
CAN MAXIMISE YOUR ABILITY TO THINK!

1. ABSORPTION

Start by fully immersing yourself in all the issues, the brand, the company, the products, the culture, the objectives, the target audience ... everything.

Try the service or buy the product to experience first hand the customer experience.

Mystery shop all the routes - web/phone/mail-order/retail shop.

Visit competitors and try their products and services.

Find out what marketing messages exist and make a list of the key ones.

Talk to customers - see who they are and what they want.

Talk to staff - internal communications are vital.

Understand the big picture - the political agenda, the key business priorities, the long term vision.

Get graduate entry packs or attend induction training.

Read TGI reports, Mintel reports, Keynote reports, get any previous research that may have been commissioned in the past.

Get all of your team involved to ensure you are gathering any prior market knowledge you have.

2. EXPLOSION - taking it 'outside the box'

There are literally hundreds of techniques that can be employed to generate new ideas (some are outlined in this section!).

But techniques are only half the story, attitudes and states of mind are equally important important.

For creativity we ensure we are:

In the right state - not in a right state. We ensure we are feeling positive, happy, optimistic, enthusiastic and brave.

Within the 'explosion' phase you must ban certain phrases: 'it won't work', 'there's no budget for that', 'we've done it before'.

3. INCUBATION

Once you have created numerous new ideas it is important to take time out to let them slosh about in your subconscious. Often ideas which initially seemed poor can morph into good ideas when left alone or allowed to merge with other thoughts. Leave them overnight on simmer!

Move on to something else. Let the knowledge just sink into your subconscious.

You will find that random thoughts and new ideas will simply spark in your mind - capture them!

4. CONSOLIDATION

At this phase take your ideas and score them against criteria that are important to you: ie. budget, can it be done in the time, does it fit the brand, communicate the key message, etc. This stage is a reality check - the ideas which can be made to work will come through. We call this filtering and it ensures that the ideas that float to the top are practical and fit for your purpose.

Note: don't dispose of the rejected ideas - keep them they may come in useful later or for another project. Create an ideas bank.

5. ACTION

It's great creating new ideas but you must put them into action. Create realistic plans and schedules so you can move things forward. The better the idea - the better the buy in from those around you. **Everyone loves to be involved in making a good idea work.**

6. CAPITALISATION

If the new ideas were linked to a commercial venture you will want to measure how much profit has been made, or there may be other measures you want to apply.

• Did it achieve the objectives?

• Did it achieve all we set out to achieve within the filters?

• What have we learnt that we could feedback into absorption?

• How can we develop our thought process?

• What did people think of it?

Try this process but if it doesn't work for you, that's OK - try something else!

This is a circular process. Once you get to point 6 you need to go back to 1 again.

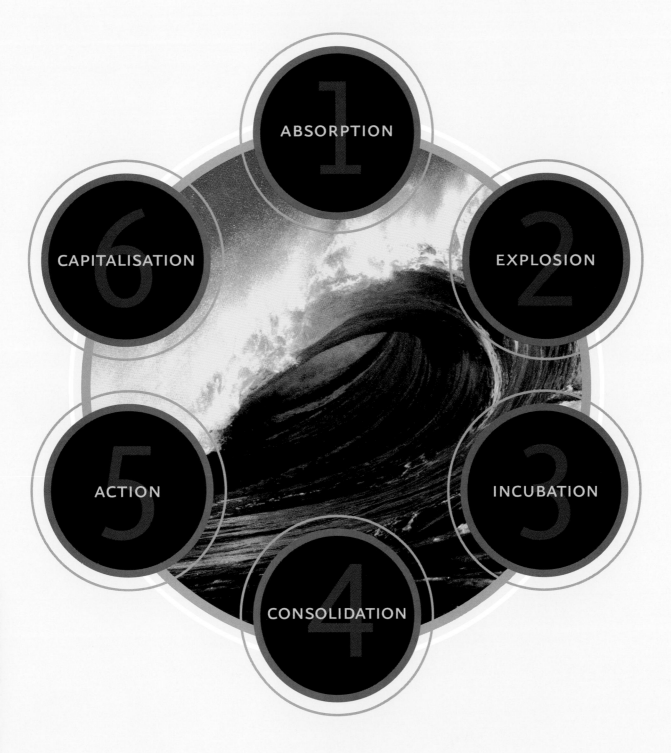

THE PROCESS

1 ABSORPTION

2 EXPLOSION

3 INCUBATION

4 CONSOLIDATION

5 ACTION

6 CAPITALISATION

YOU CAN OWN 10 SCOOTERS

BUT YOU ONLY RIDE ONE AT A TIME

CREATIVITY is about solving problems, it should be a process of refinement. The ideal is to strive for one elegant solution. Never go for the scatter-gun approach. You can have 10 ideas for a solution, but remember, you are searching for an answer, not more questions. If you are clear about your objectives the right solution will choose itself.

creativity

There are millions of people creating hundreds of ideas and yours must get through. Having the idea is not enough.

{creativity} the difference between life and death

You need to get your ideas heard and bought into.

You can plan to get the decision you want.

Here's our 5 step guide to convince others your ideas are marketable.

Step 1   Where are we now?
Step 2   Where do we want to be?
Step 3   How might we get there?
Step 4   Which way is best?
Step 5   How can we ensure we arrive?

Step 1   Where are we now?
You must clearly identify what your current position is. The starting point of this process is to provide a statement of Threats, Opportunities, Weaknesses and Strengths (always end on strengths). TOWS not SWOT. Always look at the threat of new entrants, the availability and quality of suppliers, the competition and the potential purchasers, buying patterns and capability.

Step 2   Where do you want to be?
In considering this you take the foundation from stage one and push forward.

Always start with clear objectives - make them SMART - specific, measurable, achievable, realistic and give them a timetable.

You may want to prioritise i.e. go from the most important to the least.

But state clearly and simply what you are going to achieve.

Step 3   How might we get there?
It is important to explore all the possibilities

- The new product development process
- What you have learnt from previous product successes
- The significance of price
- Methods of pricing
- Behaviour of costs over time
- The promotional plan
- The distribution plan
- The team that will do the work
- The marketing plan
- The ability of your team

To get 'buy in' for a good idea you need to prove that it is an idea that will work.

Step 4   Which way is best?
It's very difficult to know in advance what's going to happen - but you can make an educated decision. You must understand the role of criteria of choice in the decision making process. Look at the most important thing or outcome, and look at financial and non-financial criteria.

Financial criteria can be income as well as expenditure.

Non-financial criteria may examine market share or the effect on the environment, etc.

Step 5   How can you ensure you arrive?
If you are going to make it happen it's got to be controlled. Good control will help the implementation of your strategies. Getting quality feedback is essential to good control. Every stage of implementation should be the responsibility of someone.

So you can see that getting your ideas heard or bought into can be helped if you plan to get the decision you want. Just having a good idea is not enough. Make it happen.

And when you succeed - don't forget to celebrate!

conservative liberal

young old

fresh mature

soft hard

empty full

faster slower

Make a list of words connected to your

project and their opposites. Now state your

product/service using one descriptive word,

then the opposite.

design

turn it

nbɐıqɘ qoᴎu

ONE METHOD FOR CREATING NOVEL PERSPECTIVES IS

TO STATE YOUR PROBLEM OR POSITION IN THE

OPPOSITE WAY. Restaurants serve food.**Restaurants don't serve food.**

Erm - how could we make that work?

We could provide a funky trendy venue

and rent out tables for people to bring

their own food.

Or - Statement: we must improve our service

Opposite: we must worsen our service

Then list all the ways you think you

could achieve both. It's often strange to

find that our minds find the negative

more intriguing and we can easily find lists

of ways to make something worse!

Once you've gathered the negatives you

can turn them back and gain some

new positives.

Be Silly

Try looking at things from a new perspective. One of the breakthroughs in ice-cream came when the New Product Development teams stopped thinking about their product in terms of ice-cream and started to think of it as confectionery. Which opened up whole new ways of developing new product lines...

Cadburys expanded this thinking by thinking about how they could have Cadburys in every aisle of the supermarket. This expands their thinking to other categories - Cereal, Hot drinks, Ice-cream toppings, Spreads...

(Can you think of your product or service in a new frame like this?)

How you define and confine your product or service can liberate or bind you.

Think of 50 different uses for your product or service.

What is the silliest idea - could you make it work?

Our brains enjoy fun and playfulness - you can often trick your mind into doing some work by making it great fun...

If we ask ourselves what are the silliest, strangest things we could do with our product - it becomes fun.

Then we can put the ideas through a filter to consider their actual viability.

Try it!

How Creative Are You?

ANNA HARRIS

How can you measure creativity? The problem lies in the fact that creativity is an abstract concept and hence is not easily definable. Therefore, unlike concrete ideas, there is no direct method of measuring creativity. Obviously, this produces quite an obstacle for psychologists attempting to tap into these concepts. So what do we do?

Within psychology, a discipline known as psychometrics exists which allows us to create techniques for quantifying these problematic notions. The basis of psychometrics is its ability to validate tests that we generate ourselves. Essentially, statistics are applied to analyse two major criteria both of which are required in order that the technique be deemed useful. These criteria are: reliability and validity.

Reliability = a tool that accurately measures a concept.

Validity = a tool that measures the chosen concept.

Thus, a test may accurately measure something but it may not be the concept you intended. As you can see, both are needed if the test is to be applied in any situation.

So how did I apply psychometrics? I decided to choose a questionnaire format as I felt that this was an appropriate medium for measuring creativity.

Here are the stages that followed:

1 Research.
2 Item (question) design.
3 Data collection.
4 Analysis.
5 Conclusions.

RESEARCH - WHAT IS CREATIVITY?

How do you define an abstract concept? The key is research. I began by brainstorming so that I could collate ideas of specific areas of creativity e.g. music, art. However, I felt that questions relating to artistic ability, for example, would not adequately encompass what it is to be creative. Therefore I decided to turn my focus to the wealth of personality research that exists with the intention of finding traits and characteristics that tend to cluster with creativity.

One of the main exponents of personality theory was Carl Jung (a contemporary of Freud). He claimed that there were four major personality types: sensing, thinking, intuiting and feeling. We possess all of these to a greater or lesser extent but one is our 'superior function' – that which is preferred and most developed.

In 1978, Susan Dellinger took Jung's idea and expanded it to create psychogeometrics. In this system, an individual chooses a symbol (red triangle, yellow squiggle, blue square, or green circle) that best represents them. These are accompanied by a set of personality traits. According to Dellinger, 86% select the most appropriate symbol for themselves.

How does this relate to creativity? Dellinger tells us that the squiggle is the emblem of those that are most creative (this corresponds to Jung's feeling function). However, we are also told that squiggles are innovative, driven by challenges, interested in abstract concepts, unfocused, disorganised, spontaneous and risk-takers.

These ideas were supplemented by more research within personality- and creativity-based books.

QUESTIONNAIRE FORMAT

Before we could write the questionnaire, a format needed to be chosen. There are several types (such as Thurstone and Guttmann) but the most common type used within psychology is the Likert scale. This provides the participant with a range of choices according to how strongly they agree or disagree with each statement. It has generally been accepted that currently this is the best method as it allows not just an agree/disagree answer but a value given as to the strength of agreement.

However, there has been much discussion as to the most suitable number of response choices. Frequently, either five or seven choices are given (allowing for an undecided option) although some argue that more than five options can confuse participants. Therefore five choices were given next to each item: strongly agree, agree, undecided, disagree and strongly disagree. Each is given a value from one to five and the end score (how creative are you?) is the sum of these values.

ITEM DESIGN - A GAME OF 20 QUESTIONS!

The next stage was to design the items that would constitute the questionnaire. The aim was to generate quite a large number so that at least 20 of the best would remain after initial analysis. Taking the above research, I set about writing the

1 Creativity
associated with squiggles and those using the feeling function

2 Therefore
those that are creative are more likely to have other traits that are associated with squiggles

3 These traits include
innovation, imagination, orientated towards abstract concepts, unfocused, disorganisation, spontaneity, risk-taking, theatrical and obsessive

4 Creativity requires
insight into yourself and others, a good imagination, use of visual representations and a desire to communicate

HOW DOES PERSONALITY RELATE TO CREATIVITY?

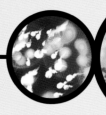

items according to the content domain (i.e. what creativity should encompass). This may seem simple but there are certain rules that are generally applied during item design so that respondents can answer the questions to the best of their ability without being biased by extraneous variables.

These include:
1. Use simple language (no jargon).
2. Do not use double-barrelled items (i.e. don't have two parts to the question).
3. Have equal numbers of positive and negative items i.e. some that tap into creativity and some that tap into non-creative traits (so that participants do not just tick all the agree responses).
4. Do not make the items too long (best to keep to around seven words).
5. Make sure they are monotonic (definitely directed at either creative or non-creative characteristics).

In total, 48 statements were composed.

PROCEDURE - RECRUITING GUINEA PIGS!

In order to find out whether our questionnaire was scientifically viable, it was essential to ask some people to complete it so that the process of validation could begin. Unfortunately, to some, this may seem an utterly boring set of tasks (especially if you are not filled with joy when the word statistics is mentioned). Regrettably however, my creative mind needed dulling for the sake of science!

We focused on three major forms of reliability and validity:

Internal Reliability - decides whether the questionnaire is internally consistent i.e. do all the questions measure the same thing. The related procedure (known as item analysis) encompasses a series of rules of thumb that allow removal of unreliable items.

Test-Retest Reliability - allows us to establish whether the questionnaire is stable over time by assessing whether a person gives significantly similar answers even after several weeks have passed.

Criterion-Related Validity - does the questionnaire actually measure the construct? This procedure compares the scores of creative people and non-creative people on the basis that if creativity is being

measured, the total scores for the two groups should significantly differ.

Additionally, another statistical technique was applied: factor analysis.

Factor Analysis - allows the data set to be reduced by showing which of the items are most strongly linked. This leaves us with clusters of items that are similar - i.e. different components of the questionnaire. This seemed particularly worthwhile, as I have always believed creativity to be a multi-faceted concept. That is, those that are good musicians are not always good artists or good with abstract concepts. We cannot afford to pigeonhole people as either creative or not as we all have our own method for expressing our creativity.

The questionnaire was sent specifically to those who are traditionally deemed as either particularly creative or non-creative. When we received the completed versions, item analysis was performed so that unreliable items were removed (this left us with 24 items). The new form was again dispatched to these same people and more statistics performed on the new set of data (notably, test-retest reliability, criterion-related validity and factor analysis).

RESULTS - DID WE FIND ANYTHING?

At this point, I'd like to thank all those lovely, patient people that agreed to help with this project (especially those that took the time to complete the questionnaire).

Now for the all-important question - what did we find?

1. Internal Reliability - we managed to reduce the questionnaire from 48 to 24 items through a process of eliminating those that did not discriminate (were not good measures). The major measure of internal reliability is Cronbach's alpha (a figure between 0-1). The closer to 1, the more internally consistent the test is.

Our final Cronbach's alpha (for 24 items) = 0.91. Therefore, our test is internally reliable.

2. Test-retest reliability

3. Criterion-related validity - when the two groups

(creative vs. non-creative) were compared on the final 24 items via a t-test, the creative group scored significantly higher than the non-creative group.

Mean of creative group = 86.0 (out of 120)
Mean of non-creative group = 76.1 (out of 120)

Therefore, criterion-related validity was achieved i.e. the questionnaire does actually measure creativity.

4. Factor analysis - five components were found. According to the items included in the factor, each was given a name. These were:

a. Imagination, thoughts and concepts - the individual often uses imagination to good effect and transposes these original ideas through metaphors and visual representations. Additionally, these people produce innovative ideas which are often based on abstract concepts. However, they are not always generated in an ordered way.

b. Artistic nature - these individuals encompass the traditional view i.e. they are very creative (generally in an artistic manner).

c. Musical and dramatic nature - these people's hobbies are often creative with particular appreciation for music and drama. They often find these to be stimulating and they may be used within a work situation.

d. Analytical nature - these individuals could be classified as thinkers as they are often inquisitive and try to provide several solutions to a problem. They are always trying to understand others and are usually good at reading emotions.

e. Flexibility in life - these individuals are not afraid to try new things and tend to have a flexible attitude to life (including within a work situation).

How Creative Are You?

ANNA HARRIS

Everyone can be creative. This survey is designed to establish your personal creativity profile.

what kind of creative are you?

The results will enable you to understand where you have creative strengths and weaknesses, and will enable you to think about developing your skills.

PLEASE CIRCLE THE APPROPRIATE NUMBER FOR EACH QUESTION AND THEN MOVE ON TO THE SELF DIAGNOSTIC SECTION ON THE NEXT PAGE.

		Strongly Agree	Agree	Undecided	Disagree	Strongly Disagree
1.	I am perceived as artistic	1	2	3	4	5
2.	I like to be creative	1	2	3	4	5
3.	I'm not a particularly flexible person	1	2	3	4	5
4.	I am not seen as an arty person	1	2	3	4	5
5.	I like to provide several solutions to a problem	1	2	3	4	5
6.	I am not seen as a very creative person	1	2	3	4	5
7.	I enjoy using my imagination	1	2	3	4	5
8.	My hobbies do not involve being creative	1	2	3	4	5
9.	I often use visual representations in my work	1	2	3	4	5
10.	I do not analyse myself often	1	2	3	4	5
11.	I easily see imagery in classical music	1	2	3	4	5
12.	I think that I am imaginative	1	2	3	4	5
13.	I do not tend to use metaphors to describe something	1	2	3	4	5
14.	I prefer working with concrete rather than abstract concepts	1	2	3	4	5
15.	I enjoy the dramatic arts	1	2	3	4	5
16.	I am always asking "What if?"	1	2	3	4	5
17.	I seek new experiences	1	2	3	4	5
18.	I do things in an ordered way	1	2	3	4	5
19.	I often produce original thoughts and ideas	1	2	3	4	5
20.	I don't try to actively understand what others are thinking	1	2	3	4	5
21.	I am not innovative	1	2	3	4	5
22.	I enjoy using abstract concepts and theories within my work	1	2	3	4	5
23.	I would find a piece of poetry in the middle of a report annoying	1	2	3	4	5
24.	I find that art and music stimulates my thinking	1	2	3	4	5

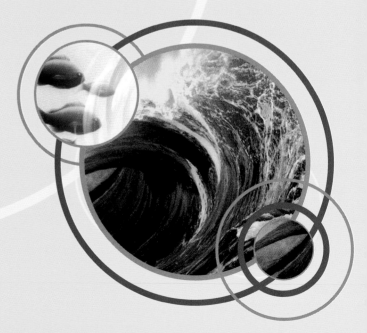

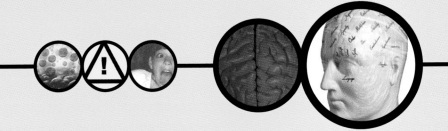

SELF-DIAGNOSTIC - TRY IT YOURSELF (YOU KNOW YOU WANT TO)

First, complete the questionnaire opposite and then add up your score according to the information below.

For each of your answers award yourself the number of points that are shown in the table.

Question	Strongly Agree	Agree	Undecided	Disagree	Strongly Disagree
1	5	4	3	2	1
2	5	4	3	2	1
3	1	2	3	4	5
4	1	2	3	4	5
5	5	4	3	2	1
6	1	2	3	4	5
7	5	4	3	2	1
8	1	2	3	4	5
9	5	4	3	2	1
10	1	2	3	4	5
11	5	4	3	2	1
12	5	4	3	2	1
13	1	2	3	4	5
14	1	2	3	4	5
15	5	4	3	2	1
16	5	4	3	2	1
17	5	4	3	2	1
18	1	2	3	4	5
19	5	4	3	2	1
20	1	2	3	4	5
21	1	2	3	4	5
22	5	4	3	2	1
23	1	2	3	4	5
24	5	4	3	2	1

For your total creativity score, just add all the points you got. From our pilot study, the average score was 81.1 points (out of a possible total of 120 points).

You can now calculate how creative you are within each of the components of the questionnaire by adding your scores for each question according to the information below.

Component	Questions
Imagination, thoughts and concepts	7, 9, 12, 13, 14, 18, 19, 21, 22.
Artistic nature	1, 2, 4, 6.
Musical and dramatic nature	8, 11, 15, 24.
Analytical nature	5, 10, 16, 20.
Flexibility in life	3, 17, 23.

The average scores for each component are shown below.

Component	Average Score	Total Score
Imagination, thoughts, concepts	29.7	45
Artistic nature	13.4	20
Musical and dramatic nature	13.4	20
Analytical nature	14.4	20
Flexibility in life	10.4	15

HOW TO IMPROVE

Well done - whatever your score, you have shown that in some way you are creative. You may not be particularly artistic but perhaps your ideas and concepts are more creative than you thought.

However, you must not forget that creativity can be learnt and improved. It just requires you to find that important bit of your brain (quite often in the right hemisphere) and make it practice (well, that is what my art teacher used to say!).

One of the major problems with those that feel they are not creative is control. Let go. Creativity is not always logical and just allowing random ideas and associations to drive your thinking can be very productive.

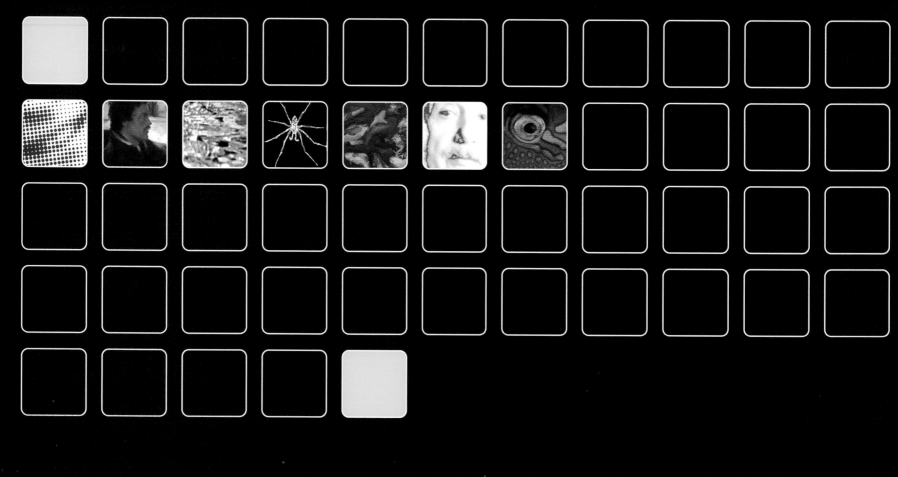

Interesting People

People are an almost infinite source of diversity and creativity. Creativity can arise from a clash of ideas or a refreshing new insight.

You must be generous and allow yourself to learn from other people - be open to new ideas and adventure into new areas - poetry, art, business, literature.

How do young people think? Are you a tenacious idea hunter?

Hopefully this section will give you an insight into a few amazing minds and will stimulate you to be open to meeting and really listening to the ideas and thought processes of others.

Learn from other people. Ask them - how do you think and what do you think?

if most people were given the task to find a needle in a haystack they would stop when they found the first needle

so einstein, tell us a little about your genius.

**Don't settle for your first idea
- the chances are it won't be
the one you are looking for!**

Einstein was once interviewed about his genius. He was asked what it was that made him different from most people. His reply was that if most people were given the task of finding a needle in a haystack, they would stop when they found the first needle. He said that, unlike 'most' people, he would keep looking until he had found *all* the possible needles.

The best way to create great ideas is to create lots of ideas, and then you can compare them and find the one that fits your needs best (don't forget you can 'bank' the others for later - they may not be the ultimate solution now but they may work another time).

If you were given the task of finding a needle in a haystack, would you stop when you found the first needle, or would you relentlessly carry on until you felt you had found all the possible needles? Don't have a lazy mind - push for the best ideas.

To create the best ideas you need to be tenacious. You need to have energy and you need to be courageous - you can do that!

Does it feel strange spending time just reading a poem at work? It is a valid use of time - you are thinking!

When was the last time you sat down (or walked around) and read a piece of poetry? Creative writing, like art and music, can trigger random new ideas in your head that you can relate to your area of business. Read this poem and write down any links you can make to give you ideas (i.e. list words from the chosen poem that could link to your project).

Conspicuous Consumption

A fairly large spider just crawled
down the kitchen wall. Only eight
inches from my face, I can see him
most clearly. His wiggly bits,
wiggling.

I am not frightened of spiders so
asked him how he was, blew him
a soft breath. An over-reaction then,
to fall out of sight - where I don't know.

I have looked under the table, on
the floor, behind the radiator. He
was in no danger. I like spiders.
Might have done with

a bit of succour, those love pads.
But the dull beat of his fear
dropped out of sight at my
sigh of recognition.

Come, climb on my back, tap, tap,
tap on the puckered thread of
my resistance. Soon we will
dance anew, soon the beat will
drive a fresh hunger.

Claire Archibald

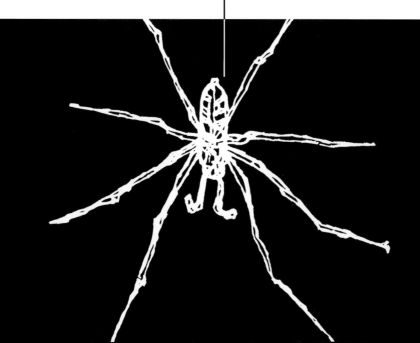

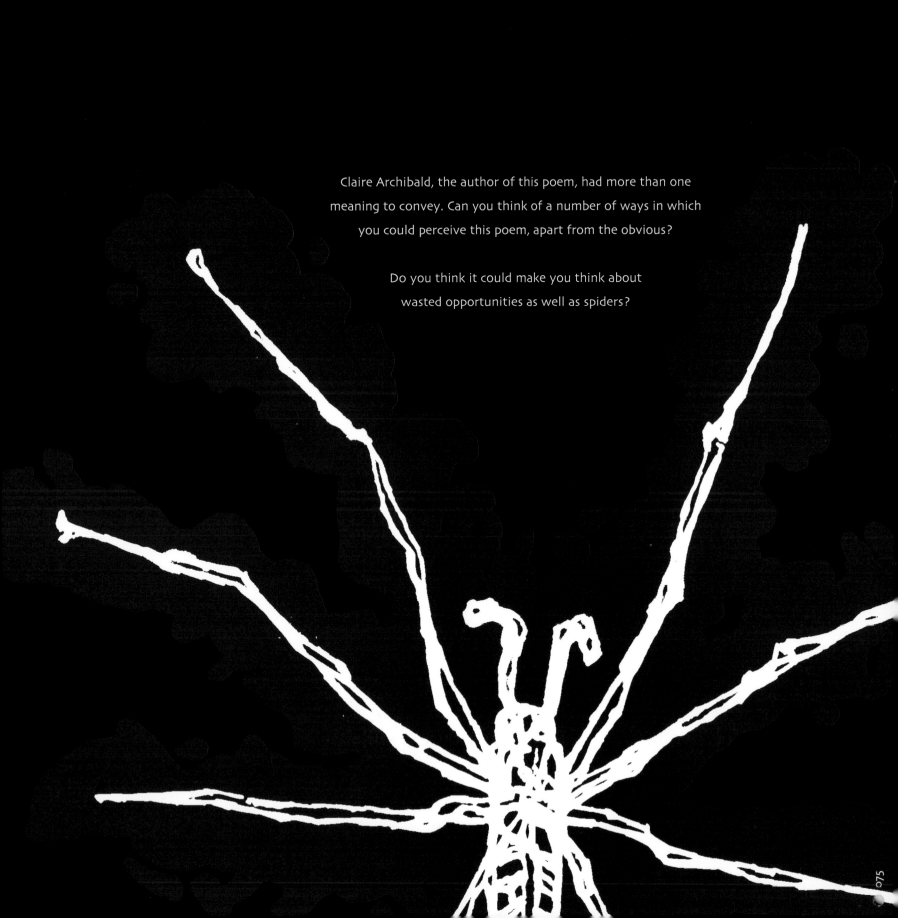

Claire Archibald, the author of this poem, had more than one meaning to convey. Can you think of a number of ways in which you could perceive this poem, apart from the obvious?

Do you think it could make you think about wasted opportunities as well as spiders?

075

A day with Sir Tom Farmer was a unique and stimulating experience.

"What is the most important question in management?" This is the cunningly simple question we were asked when we first visited Sir Tom Farmer at his Kwik Fit head office in Edinburgh.

"What do you think?"

?

outside the box had won Sir Tom as a prize. That is to say that *outside the box* had been fortunate enough to win a coveted prize as one of the companies most likely to thrive in the new millennium. We won a special category prize for our unique initiatives to keep our teams happy and motivated. The category was Investors in People and part of the prize was a day with Sir Tom Farmer, Chief Executive of Kwik Fit. As it turned out, this was the most valuable prize we could have won, better than the plaque for the wall, better even than the cash. A day with Sir Tom Farmer was a unique and stimulating experience, which has provided us with a friend and mentor for life.

Do you have a special mentor? Someone you admire and can learn from - if not think about it. Who would you learn from most?

We were very anxious to meet the man who had built his company from nothing and sold it to Ford for more than one billion pounds. What could we ask him that would help us learn, how would we need to address him? How should we prepare?

We needn't have been concerned. Sir Tom arranged for us to be met at Edinburgh station and take us to his offices. His warm and delightfully professional PA met us and showed us into the Kwik Fit boardroom. We were offered tea and as we looked around we noticed a strange standard lamp that was made out of an exhaust pipe (of course)!

Tom, as we are now privileged to know him, strode into the room with the confidence that you would expect from a successful man at the top of his career. Then he beamed a warm smile and asked us to tell him all about *us* and *our* company. It was humbling as Sir Tom Farmer listened intently - then he asked us …

"What do you think is the most important question in business?"

Oh dear - and it had been going so well up to that point. Mark and I looked at each other searching for the best answer we could come up with. But before he let us suffer he kindly replied to his own question. With a wry cheeky smile Sir Tom said

"What do you think?"

"That's it," he said. "That is the most important question in business."

This was the first of many insights into the extraordinary thinking of a man who started by cleaning cookers and who is now a multi-millionaire. His wisdom is so strikingly simple that it leaves you wondering why it is that so many managers and management consultants have such trouble getting to the simplicity but, as Sir Tom says, "the bigger a company gets the dumber it gets".

So, Think! And learn what other people Think! Be brave, be generous and wake up your brain. This takes courage and you need to be prepared to take a few personal risks but it is worth it. Today we all need to really use as much of our thinking capacity as we can. To drift along not stepping into uncharted territory will get you nowhere. You need to plan, to think of new ideas, be innovative, be challenging, be bold and be brave.

Whether you are a student, a teacher, a manager, a parent, a politician, a gardener, a poet, a painter or are just running a multi-million multinational corporation, like Sir Tom, you need to Think!

Our brains love to be lazy and take the easy route - don't let them. Get control and try some new ways of thinking - give your brain a work out - NOW!

Forget what they did to you at school - you **are** fantastically creative.

Forget about the culture at work - you **can** be innovative and challenge the givens.

Everyone has the capacity to be creative, you may have just forgotten how to do it.

First, we all need to be a little kinder, firstly to ourselves (aren't those little voices in your head always telling you to give up on thinking - do they tell you that you are not creative or innovative?). Just tell them to Shut Up! **You are** in charge now and **you are** creative.

Next we need to be kind to our families, friends and colleagues. We need to be generous and listen to the ideas of others. No matter how ridiculous you may think an idea sounds at first give it space - ideas are like candles, they can be snuffed out if they have no oxygen.

"I don't sit and look at an empty table and become inspired. It's people that inspire me. People talking, listen, sometimes you just notice there is a flow. For example 'You can't get better than a Kwik Fit fitter!' was created one night when we were all talking about how "it's the fitters that people deal with, they are the ones who do the work and... 'you can't get better than a Kwik Fit fitter'. "

Nothing

Sir Tom Farmer

"I listen to other people and gather thoughts and ideas and I lock those thoughts in to my head. I don't know at the time how those thoughts might come in useful. Then, as time passes I will be thinking about something else and I recall something - it's not a conscious process - it floats up."

"I am a collector of ideas, everything and anything. I think 'What can I do with what I've heard?' or 'How can I use what I've seen?'

People are my inspiration - there is a buzz when people are all supporting each other and generating ideas. Once you let your imagination go... it's incredible. When we were growing Kwik Fit we would get together sometimes on a Saturday or Sunday morning and just have lots of ideas - we didn't allow 'stinking thinking' - you know the sort of thinking that doubts and questions and pulls everyone down."

comes from nothing

I need to work with people with energy and people who
I feel comfortable with - people on the same wavelength.

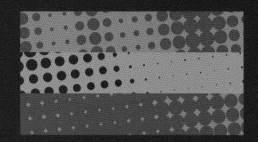

" I sponsored some of David Mach's work and I came to know him. He took me around an art gallery and showed me three stripes on a canvas - he explained it was a woman eating a melon. I didn't see it until he went through the thought process from the original work which looked like a woman eating a melon to the final three stripes. The process was more interesting than the final product for me. You need to remain inquisitive and open minded to new ways of looking at things. **"**

To encourage creativity you have to have the courage to allow room in your organisation for individuality.

You have to be very careful you are not taking away people's creativity.

I used to think management was like being a conductor for a classical orchestra but now I think of it more in terms of conducting a jazz band. Everyone in the band knows they need to play within a framework for the result to sound good but every night individuals can adapt what they play and be creative and individual.

Another way to look at managing for creativity is to think of the team within an elastic band - they can push and stretch it in lots of ways and as long as they don't stretch it 'til breaking point then it's great.

Be aware of systems and procedures - too much detail can screw you up.

When we first began Kwik Fit, we had 2 sides of A4 to run a depot then later we needed an A5 booklet.

Recently I discovered we had a 75-page manual. It is important to create structure but if you go too far with bureaucracy you take away an individual's need to think (and nobody reads 50 pages anyway!)

Be careful that your team are not so busy doing compulsory staff assessments or form filling that they forget they are supposed to be servicing the customer.

I can walk into a Kwik Fit depot and I just know if it's all working as it should do - that comes from intuition.

Intuition is years of experience. Gut feel - that's just indigestion.

I have a digital camera and if I go out I take it with me - I take pictures which help to remind me of what I've seen and they give me ideas on how we could improve. On a visit recently I ended up doing 3 hours of fitting myself - going 'back to the floor' is also a really important way to think about your business.

Stimulate, support, challenge, courage - intuition

Pay attention all the time to bring in the best people, and make sure they have a 'can do' attitude - without this all the thinking in the world won't make things happen.

Recently we launched a campaign to improve our business. We asked our most experienced managers to take 9 centres each and take 10 things and make it happen - within the broad framework how they were to actually do the work was up to them - **flexibility allows creativity.**

If you want to consider creativity ask yourself who are the most creative people you know?

6 year olds! - they are not afraid to try and they don't mind failure.

When I have an idea then it is important to explain it and share it with others. I use metaphors and stories to explain my ideas - because then everyone understands.

Make sure you support people and make them feel human - remember there is a lot going on in people's lives - we can't all perform 100% every day.

If someone is a crook, a villain or lazy - I can't support them but if someone honestly tries their best and fails - fine, I can help. Inspiration, not salvation, is what we can realistically achieve.

> **"Intuition is years of experience. Gut feel - that's just indigestion."**

James Davies

JAMES DAVIES

is a 15 year old pupil
@ Cardinal Hean
High School, Leeds

THINKING ABOUT THINKING @ FIFTEEN

From the outside most high schools look no less than ideal; hundreds of uniformed students begin every school day carrying all their school books and are eager to get inside to meet friends and have some fun, the teachers friendly but always in control, and a great sense of community within the school that binds the separate groups together. Students receive a broad education and are provided with enough free time to help them survive the day. Yet despite this idyllic appearance, students find it hard to learn or to pay attention because of the boring, repetitive nature that is necessary in many lessons because of the great emphasis placed on test results. These tests restrict students from learning things simply for the enjoyment value, and instead put great pressure on pupils and teachers alike to work countless hours to achieve the best grades. This not only puts students under a great strain, but also discourages them from actually wanting to learn for themselves.

The broad range of subjects and the inability to drop those that you don't like causes further problems: you have future artists being forced to learn the intricacies of modern physics, potential builders trying to memorise Mark's gospel, and upcoming hairdressers trying pitifully to play the recorder in seemingly endless music lessons. This situation is as hopeless in practice as it is in theory, and it results in high school becoming a place to endure, rather than enjoy.

An individual's independence does not have a place in high school. In classes of up to thirty-four, it is nearly impossible for the teacher to remember everybody's name, never mind a person's personality, strengths and weaknesses, or even their ability. This lack of detailed recognition between pupil and teacher hinders the learning process by not allowing teachers to anticipate any problems that a pupil may experience, and thirty-four teenagers in a class is a daunting prospect for anyone who wants to raise their hand and ask a question. And so, in this difficult situation, individualism is simply inconvenient, and a class can usually only be taught as a whole, oblivious to any person's particular needs.

It is understandable then, that in this already hectic environment, teachers have very little time to discuss and teach anything as trivial as thinking, or even put some time aside for a regular debate about the subjects we have

been studying. Few teachers dare to venture out of the familiar teaching patterns to try anything new. The frantic, revision-packed lessons are grimly accepted by the pupils who gradually grow to accept the fact that this is the way they should always learn. It is no surprise then, with the great pressure placed upon teachers and students to get good results, that school becomes an environment in which adding your opinion without being asked, or questioning what is being taught, is looked upon as being bad mannered. I am of course speaking very generally, and it is true that some teachers do break away from the normal teaching patterns to provide a new, refreshing approach to learning. The majority of these new methods are extremely effective and also make the class a more enjoyable and successful place to study, and therefore receive a greater response from the pupils than ordinary, monotonous lessons. Things as simple as group discussions, class presentations, short-term projects or even something as potentially patronizing as a chocolate reward for the best work can serve to motivate and encourage an entire class to work.

High school is a good place to learn, but its teaching is limited. There is very little beyond the everyday academia of retaining facts and figures, and rather than teaching students how to think and learn for themselves, they are merely taught the information necessary to get good results. Many students come out with the results that they immediately need in order to follow the path they wish to take, but very few leave school with a greater knowledge of how to think creatively and challenge existing ideas - knowledge that will be useful long after the GCSE results are forgotten.

alan flood

As a practising artist, one of the most valuable lessons I have learned is that of the importance of dreaming. Whilst having some sort of plan or preconceived idea, I have realised that there has to be fluidity in one's understanding in order to allow for a change of direction and the blending of new ideas. In this mind state (described by some as free-flow thinking) one is open to new possibilities where anything in one's environment can act as a catalyst: TV, film, text, physical surface, trace of memory, a sound or a smell.

An artist who is a brilliant example of this kind of thinking is the Spanish painter Pablo Picasso. To quote him "I don't borrow I steal." He devoured the world around himself; even other artist's work, and even when taking other people's ideas he completely digested them and made them his own.

Often the painted portrait can provide an insight into this creative way of thinking and working. With a portrait the artist is not merely providing a photographic likeness but he or she is giving a poetical and emotional insight into the sitter as subject. To quote Picasso again "If all an artist is, is an eye, then he is an imbecile." A conversation is set up between the artist, the sitter and the painting itself. The subject makes certain demands on the artist but also so does the painting. This produces a sort of balancing act between all three elements. A successful portrait is a good likeness and a good painting.

ALAN FLOOD

1 'Koi' (previous spread)
Acrylic on panel 111.5 x 119.5

2 'Waiting'
Oil on canvas 107x107cm

3 Alan Flood's studio

4 'Vanitas' Still Life
Oil on Panel, 41 x 46cm

alan flood

4

Alan Flood was born in Blackburn, Lancashire. He studied at Blackburn School of Art and The School of Fine Art, Leeds Polytechnic. After a successful career as an illustrator he returned to full-time painting in 1987. His subjects range from portrait and group figure compositions to still life and interiors. He now lives and works in Leeds as a full-time painter.

"Few occupations are so important to the well-being of society than that of the artist who makes something that was not there before which can enhance our comprehension of and delight in our world and ourselves."

Mary Sara, curator & art critic

The importance of the arts in the process of recovery has long been recognised. In the 18th century, Handel played to patients and Hogarth painted murals in hospital buildings. Present day scientific research supports the case for providing "harmonious environments" for the process of healing, and various controlled projects demonstrate a reduction in patient stress, a lowered requirement for drugs and faster recuperation rates. In mental health the use of art in promoting effective

coping strategies and enhancing personal growth is now receiving a great deal more attention. Recent years have seen a

variety of initiatives which place the arts as central to health promotion and the delivery of comprehensive health

services. "Art works in mental health" is one example of a partnership of national organisations involved in mental

health. It is currently involved in a campaign to showcase the many creative talents processed by those with mental

health problems. The council for music in hospitals is a charity that brings the therapeutic benefit of live music to adults

and children with all kinds of illness, mental health problems, learning and physical abilities.

Fred Wright
Consultant Clinical Psychologist

" We all make a personal journey through life, a journey of discovery, sometimes fraught with danger, difficulty or breakdown, sometimes enlivened by colour, excitement and adventure. Creativity itself is an odyssey which entails struggle, whether we are creating our own life history or creating a work of art. "

Psychoanalysis developed as "the talking cure" for people with emotional and mental health problems. But it has a lot to say to healthy people as well about how our minds may work and how we think - productively and unproductively.

Freud developed a technique for exploring aspects of the mind not always accessible to conscious thought through hypnosis and then through free association. In this way he developed theories of mind eg. a mind composed of instinct or emotion (the id), of conscience (supergo) and of reality sense (ego) often in conflict. He also conceived the idea of a developmental aspect of the mind linked to developing sexuality (oedipal and preoedipal) and ideas about the psychopathology of development occurring through defensive strategies in thinking which protect the mind from internal and external trauma.

Analysts who came after Freud developed these ideas. One of the most influential was Melanie Klein and she and those who worked with her enabled the development of ideas about mental processes, how we think, perceive the world, and learn, or fail to learn, from experiences. Psychoanalysis as a psychological treatment helps people to develop freer, more organised or more creative thinking and be released from rigid thinking or chaotic, unboundaried thought.

From these ideas we can begin to conceptualise blocks to original thought.

Repression: (Freud)
Unwanted thought or ones that are difficult to accept as ones own and assimilate are pushed down into the unconscious like drowning a puppy. These thoughts struggle to find expression but cannot be fully expressed. And so pieces of the jigsaw puzzle are lost, full understanding or integrated experience does not happen and creative energy is lost and used up in the struggling of the unconscious thoughts for survival.

Splitting: (Klein, Fairbairne)
When feelings are intense, as they are for instance for a frightened frustrated or hungry baby, then primitive or simplistic methods are sought by the mind to deal with this situation. Thoughts, feelings, ideas get polarised into good and bad (or evil), black and white. It seems to be dangerous or repulsive to contemplate shades of grey. And the different experiences are well apart so one idea cannot be influenced by another to create a mix of thoughts which can grow and change. Of course some polarisation is helpful in clarifying ideas but not if this goes on indefinitely. This process, if it goes on too long and feelings are not resolved, can become infused with different sorts of aggression including envy and other destructive wishes so that thinking becomes increasingly damaged or fragmented and all that is available is disjointed psychotic-like thought.

Containment: (Bion)
Bion developed an elaborate system to describe evolving thought and its different elements. One of his central ideas was that for people to learn to manage their thoughts and feelings so as to have an active, lively, receptive capacity to think they need to experience being in the presence of another who handles and contains their anxiety. A parent, for instance, with a young child will listen to cries and complaints and not overreact with their own anxiety but digest the anxiety, make it more understandable, respond lovingly to the child's hateful feelings. Within the relationship something happens. Anxiety settles and out of this situation thinking and understanding takes place within the containment of the vessel of the relationship. In time individuals learn the process of soothing themselves and containing their own anxiety and thus self-regulating emotions.

Symbolisation: (Segal)
Also a follower of Klein, Segal was interested in how children developed symbolic thinking through play. She thought that in psychosis (and perhaps in children learning to develop their thinking) an image may come to represent something and thus convey meaning ie. symbolise something, or it may be thought to be identical to that something in which case the perception is a delusion or hallucination. This second process may occur when a person cannot separate the difference between me and not me, my thought about a situation and the situation itself. There are aspects of omnipotence and control. She describes this situation as symbolic equation where productive thought cannot really take place, there are no links between different ideas which might produce a train of thought that would lead somewhere new. Imagination has no fluidity, no uncertainty, it is static and fundamentally meaningless to anyone else but the person having the thought. To develop symbolic thinking requires the person to be able to tolerate separation, difference and the loneliness that brings and may entail painful re-evaluation of thoughts.

Celly Rowe
Consultant Psychiatrist and Psychotherapist

During 2001 the Royal College of Psychiatrists launched what was called its Mind Odyssey project. This was essentially a celebration of the arts, psychiatry and the mind. Mental Health Services throughout the country were encouraged to organise artistic events in keeping with the project's objectives. Already there have been a great many events including "An evening of classical Urdu poetry", "Psychiatrists playing Jazz"; The Mind Odyssey film festival and "Face It", an exhibition of self-portraits, to name but a few.

The Leeds response to the Odyssey invitation was to organise a week of varied artistic events during June 2002.

It was agreed that the week would involve the full range of visual and performing arts, the spoken word, drawing and painting, dance, drama, music and poetry. It displayed works of art by a variety of people including staff who work in mental health services, those who have suffered mental ill health and those who are either professional artists or who use artistic expression as part of their leisure activity. The week focused on the promotion of various aspects of mental health and its links with the arts; the arts as a way of understanding the mind; the value of creativity as a protection of good mental health; and the importance of the healing qualities of the arts. Its potential importance for individuals is vividly illustrated by this quote from someone with mental health difficulties.

II Photography is my new coping strategy and the therapy that helps keep the dark moods of depression at bay. It is also a fantastic way of easing the stress and anxiety I find so hard to control. I cannot overstate the sense of achievement and pleasure I derive from producing a good picture. To capture a unique moment in a split second is an awesome experience. II

(Breakthrough Volume 6 Issue 6)

The success of the Odyssey week in Leeds will be measured by our future capacity to explore the many opportunities artistic expression can generate for those wishing to sustain positive mental health or recover from mental ill health. It requires us to maximise the connections between those with artistic talents and those yet to explore the creative side of themselves. It was Mary Barnes who described her personal journey through mental ill health and her redemption through painting and writing. Her story "The Hollow Tree", which dates from the 60s, is particularly poignant and demonstrates the resilience of the human spirit and the place that writing can hold in describing one's emotions.

the hollow tree

There was once a tree in the forest who felt very sad and lonely for her trunk was hollow and her head was lost in the mist.

Sometimes the mist seemed so thick that her head felt divided from her trunk. To the other trees, she appeared quite strong, but rather aloof for no wind ever sent her branches to them. She felt if she bent she would break, yet she grew so tired of standing straight.

So it was with relief that in the mighty storm she was thrown to the ground. The tree was split, her branches scattered, her roots torn up and her back was charred and blackened. She felt stunned and though her head was clear of the mist, she felt her sap dry as she felt her deadness revealed when the hollow of her trunk was open to the sky.

The other trees looked down and gasped, and didn't know whether to turn their branches politely away or whether to try to cover her emptiness and blackness with their green and brown.

The tree moaned for her own life and feared to be suffocated by theirs. She felt she wanted to lay bare and open to the wind and rain and the sun and that in time she would grow up again, full and brown, from the ground.

So it was that with the wetness of the rain she put down new roots, and by the warmth of the sun she stretched forth new wood.

In the wind her branches bent to other trees and as their leaves rustled and whispered in the dark and in the light, the tree felt loved, and laughed with life.

Mary Barnes

Case Studies

In an advertising agency, working across a broad range of businesses means that we have to be 'mental athletes'. Literally in one working day we have to create ideas for sectors as diverse as medical instrument manufacturing, chocolate retailing, fashion, construction, computer software and publishing.

This section gives you a few case studies demonstrating different thinking methodologies that may inspire you to think in different ways.

first aspirin Felix Hoffman & Heinrich Dresser
1899

first type of asprin created 1899

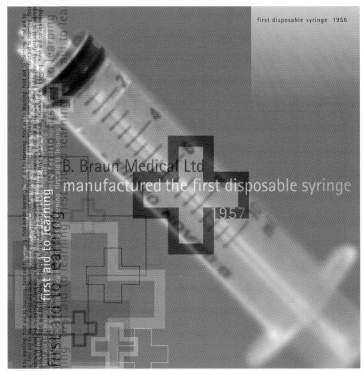

first disposable syringe 1956

B. Braun Medical Ltd
manufactured the first disposable syringe
1957

first casualty department 1962

first Casualty Department 1962
first aid to learning

James Blundell
first successful human blood transfusion
between 1825 and 1830

first blood transfusion circa 1825

B.Braun Aesculap

needed to raise

awareness of their

product offering in the

Accident & Emergency

procurement environment.

RAISING THE BLOOD PRESSURE IN A&E

In addition to a promotion which offered free educational material to B.Braun Aesculap customers, we designed a series of twelve postcards which featured high points and key events in the history of medicine.

The challenge was to create a series of impactful and retainable pieces which Accident & Emergency departments would remember and covet, lifting B.Braun Aesculap as a brand, and - in conjunction with other material - having a strong impact on sales.

This diverse series of postcards, through abstract imagery, totally relevant events and clean sharp design, became a collection that Accident & Emergency departments would really want to retain and collect.

If you were to summarise or condense the high points or key events for your product or service, what images would you choose? Try to think of four. How could you use these unique moments to create new ideas?

Milky Moo

Don't just sit there

When asked by a division of Cadbury Schweppes to consider new toppings for ice-cream, we didn't just sit and stare at the desk. We went and bought several litres of ice-cream and hundreds of sweets. We tried every sweet and combination of sweets sprinkled on the ice-cream and, to get another perspective, we invited lots of kids to join us to try the different toppings. We listened to their views about what was ugh and what was yum! What could you actively do to get a new perspective on your product or service?

Billy Blue

Honey Buzzy

The result was JoJo's, a new topping for ice-cream, desserts and cereal.

When you are asked to think of new ideas try to be active about the possible solutions. This action can give you a different perspective and a deeper understanding of what would work and what wouldn't.

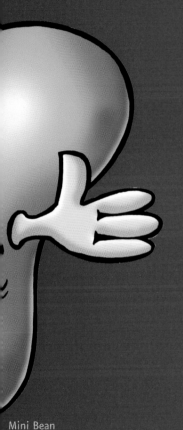

do something

Get out and ask people for their views

Buy some product and play mix 'n' match

Wear it, eat it, spray it, whatever you do try it out and try new combinations

Mini Bean

Dainty Dolly

The characters you see here are the ones we created for each flavour

Thinking about image selection can help stimulate new thinking for your project.

outside the box created a suite of photographic images that were descriptive of and covered all the main business areas in which npower, the UK's leading energy company works, including retail, hotel and catering, agriculture, medical and motoring. The images were shot with a strong 'lifestyle' feel and have a unique quality in terms of colour and movement that, in association with npower's clean and well structured graphic style, reinforces its brand position and perception among its customer base and business in general.

Thinking about image selection can help stimulate new thinking for your project.

Try thinking about what diverse range of imagery you could have in your imaginary photo library. Start with the most obvious images first and then work towards more obscure imagery.

For example, if you were selling CDs...

Start with an image of a CD then work on musicians, sound waves, relaxation, dancing, ears etc. The broader the range of images you can create the more chance you have of creating a novel insight or idea.

FACT creativity in marketing demands that everything you do is relevant to your business objective and your target audience. So wherever your creativity may take you, it's vital that you return to this fact to ensure that you achieve what you set out to achieve.

put a chicken on your head

Gerald and Maureen - big performers in incentives

outside the box were briefed by Argos Business Solutions to develop a concept and strategy for their rewards and incentives solution.

The concept had to be adaptable across a wide product range, a hugely diverse target market, and be flexible enough to work over time no matter how the market changed.

It also had to build a unique brand that would be instantly recognisable as Argos Business Solutions. The creative solution was a pair of over-the-top characters, Gerald and Maureen, who get into all sorts of situations which allow them to be the perfect carrier for the proposition. As the concept rolls out, more characters can be thrown into the equation, giving infinitely more possibilities and opportunities to demonstrate the products and their benefits.

Characters can be a good method for thinking about your product or service. Think how you would describe the person or people that are your brand.

Would they be young, old, fun, conservative, outrageous?

What would they wear?

What are their hobbies?

What car do they drive?

What paper do they read?

Once you have created your characters think of some things they might do in their spare time. Of course, incentives experts such as Gerald and Maureen spend their time having fun trying out all the new things they bought from Argos!

If you can create characters you may find they are useful in your marketing campaigns either externally, or internally to your teams.

Or they might just make you understand your product or service better.

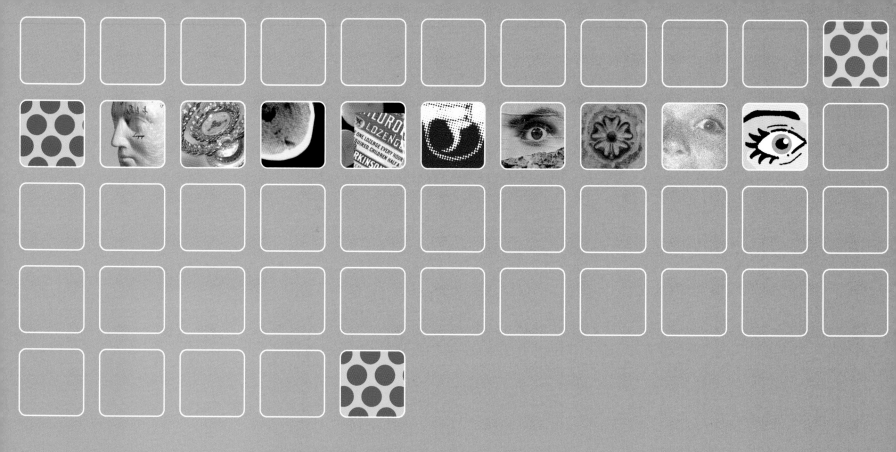

Mental

What is the difference between our minds and our brains? When nothing physically moves, what is it we feel when we are thinking hard? Our minds are amazing – this section offers you a few ideas that will stimulate your thinking and stretch your perceptions. Creativity – is it all in the mind?

Intelligence is not enough! You need to actively think!

Stop what you are doing now and think of something completely different.

This book is not here to give you academic indepth information on your brain (there are many more books on this subject). It is merely our intention to remind you to use your brain more actively - shake it up, stimulate it, metaphorically give it a workout and a cold shower. Like any muscle you are not used to consciously using you have to begin by actively thinking so you know how that feels.

'Think about a spotty blue cat negotiating its way across a purple rhubarb field that has a big green dog in it.'

Did you create a picture? Were you aware of using your brain to consider the novel situation?

Your mind is very powerful and very creative, if you don't get in its way.

You know that dogs aren't green and cats aren't blue or spotty but your mind can create a wonderful three-dimensional colour image of just those things if you let it.

It is important to tell yourself before considering this page that *this technique is an accepted and proper method for creative thinking*. You must allow yourself to put away any doubts or fears about being absolutely ridiculous in your thinking - *it is important to have crazy, zany thoughts*. It may be difficult at first, but with practice you can get there and it's worth the effort. Many great ideas have come from allowing crazy thoughts the space to develop.

Without 'crazy thinking' the telephone, the car and the light bulb would not exist. People once thought these ideas were absurd.

Edward DeBono imagined a world where anything could happen. In this world it was absurd every day and so it was easier to allow the strange and unfamiliar to occur. He called this world 'Po' - what would yours be called?

BE ABSURD

Cows can fly
Restaurants don't serve food
The grass is multicoloured
Dogs can talk
Fish fly
How crazy could you allow your imaginary world to get? Now take each of the ideas and turn them into a real, applied new thought.

The Grass is Multicoloured
Why is our grass always green when we can get flowers in thousands of colours? Perhaps the ability to have a multicoloured lawn would open up some amazingly creative horticultural schemes!

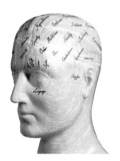 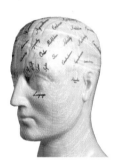 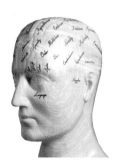 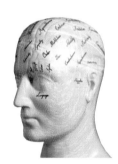 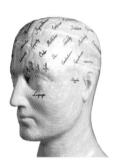 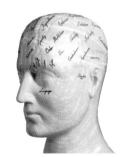

We are taught in school that day-dreaming is bad - in fact it is

an excellent thinking technique. Indulge every day if you can.

You may have to practice as it really does seem taboo at first.

Sit there, relax, look out of the window, take a deep breath and really let your mind wander.

Imagine... dream...

Einstein famously came up with his theory of relativity by imagining himself riding on a beam of light off into infinity. He was day-dreaming. Day-dreaming is a profitable pursuit!

Think.... I wonder and... why not...

Day-dreaming opens up the door to your subconscious mind. You are relaxed and in an altered state, the noises and stresses of the day are faded out. Let your mind literally wander, allowing new, fresh thoughts to emerge and develop. It takes practice because it often feels as if we are not being productive when we day-dream (actually, it often feels as if it is wrong or naughty!).

Use day-dreaming as a safe place to imagine and visualise outrageous outcomes - enormous success, global recognition, the difficult problem solved, huge wealth. But be careful what you dream of... it may come true.

Be a sponge

Be open to all the
stimulus around you
– everything can help you

Look at everything

wonder at its structure

its material

its purpose

its place

WHAT

A STATE

Being in the right state is critical to creativity. How you feel physically directly relates to your ability and capacity to think expansively and creatively. Luckily you can change your state by changing what you are doing in your mind.

Alter the state of your mind

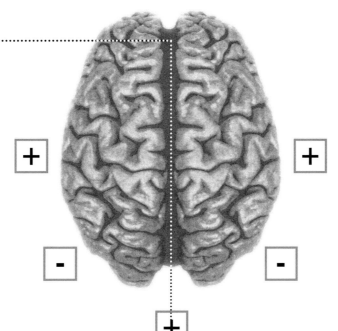

An ideal state for creative thinking would be:

Positive + Calm + Ambitious + Clear + Enthusiastic + Motivated + Happy + Relaxed + Comfortable + Confident

Think of things or situations that make you feel these things. Use them to change your state if you need to. You will find it much harder to think well if you are:

Stressed + Angry + Frustrated + Uncomfortable + Down

Before you try to Think! think about how you are feeling first. If you are not in the right state your thinking will be a lot harder.

Think about your body. If you change your physical state it helps to change your mental state.

What is the body language of someone who is on fire with ideas, animated, laughing - really enjoying the moment? And what is the body language of someone who is depressed, low, sad and lacking confidence?

Think about that and see if you can use any of these images to change your state now.

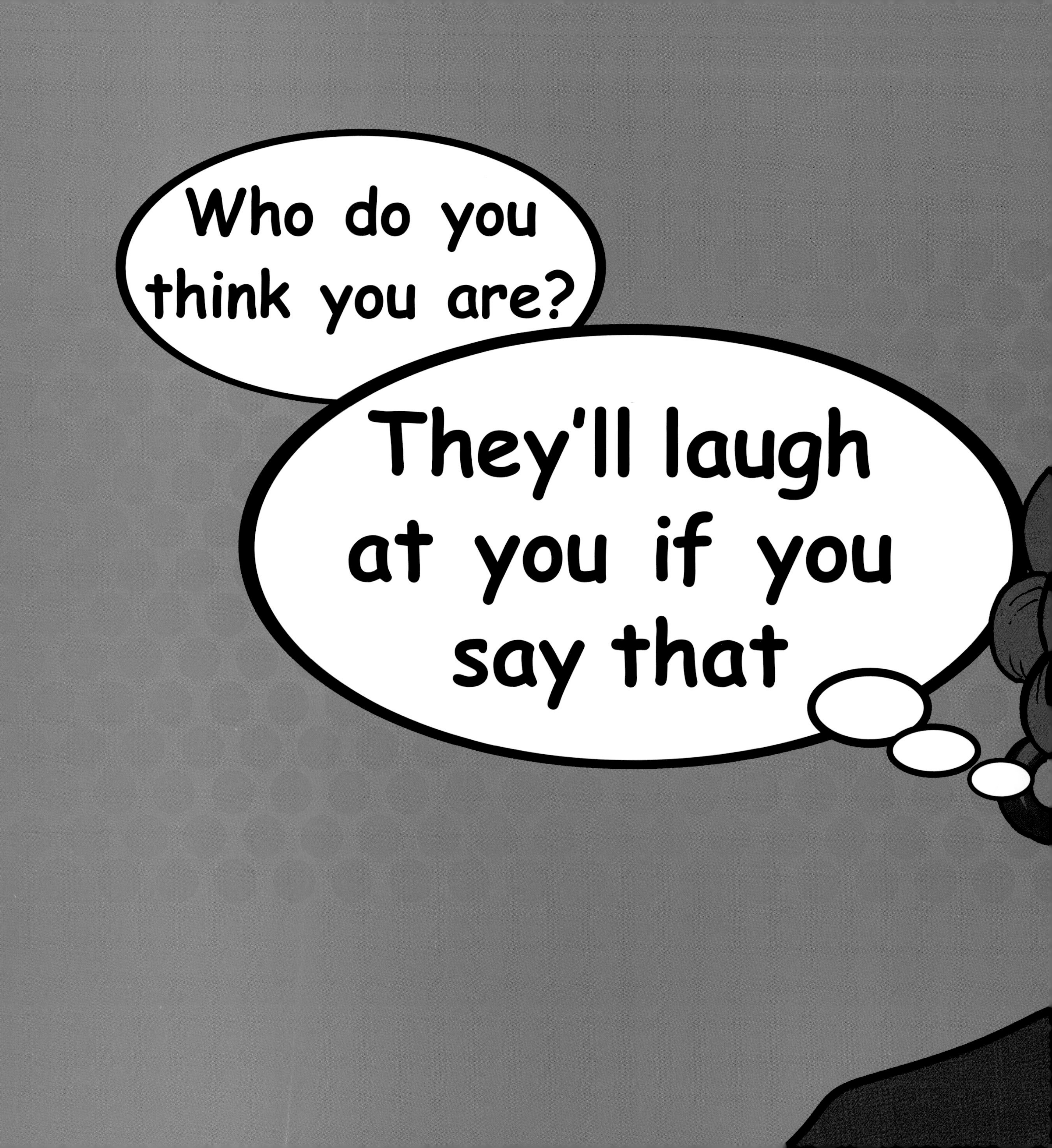
Who do you think you are?
They'll laugh at you if you say that

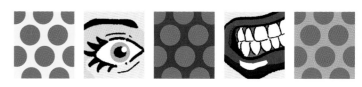

Do you ever notice
that you have voices in your head?

You're not crazy, we all have. The important thing is
to be aware of what you say to yourself!

Don't shout or be critical - be kind and give yourself
a break!

A critical, sarcastic voice can destroy your ideas.
"That's an awful idea..."
"You aren't creative..."
"Who do you think you are..."
"They'll laugh at you if you say that..."

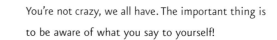

No, just stop it!

Change the tone and change the text. Next time
you are challenged to create some new thinking
- try a new voice.

"Well. it can't hurt to try."
"Why not? I'll just say it and get the feedback."
"Go on - be brave - it's a great idea."

This is so simple and so powerful. Just try it.

Think of the issue you need new ideas for and then look at a number of diverse images.

Relate the images to the need and see if you can spark new thoughts.
Hold the issue you want a new perspective on in your head and run it past each of these images:

Balloons (fun, colour, shape, occasion)

Cactus (prickly, harsh, natural, survivor)

Baby (needy, soft, cute)

image surfing

Actively think if any of these random associations spark new ideas or directions of thought for you.

comfortable

Give your brain a workout! Look at these images and words. When you do, it feels odd - you can almost feel your mind trying to access its databases for logical links. When these associations are not immediately obvious then your mind has to work harder - it has to be creative and construct meaning. Humans learn through paradox; it makes us create solutions.

Try using random words and then associate them to your product or service - the new links can often spark an idea.

antelope

omelette

erogenous

DO IT NOW!

Have you ever noticed that you sometimes have your best ideas when you are under pressure? Humans are well equipped to deal with thinking fast when they have to, and sometimes this can be useful for creative thinking.

When a deadline is looming and the pressure is building up we simply focus and get the job done. It is this focus and urgency combined that sharpens our thought processes. We do not have the luxury to research many alternatives and allow our thoughts to incubate - we have to think now!

Try creating as many novel ideas as you can in a short period of time. Within one minute, consider as many implications as you can of dogs having two heads. Did you think of novel things or did you blank? Practice in thinking fast is great mental exercise and it's fun.

Physical

Remembering your physical state of mind at a time of high achievement will naturally help to put you in the right mental state of mind. Recalling a successful moment fills you with confidence serving as a reminder that - yes you can do it! Now do it again!

Think about this:

We need thinking in order to make even better use of information that is also available to our competitors.
Edward de Bono

Stand in a beautiful
cathedral with light
streaming through
the windows

The environment you are in can dramatically alter how you think

Sit in an oak-
panelled boardroom
with green leather chairs

Walk around a lake in Spring

Smell a rose

4 these walls

Decide what environment would help you most with the ideas you need to create.

Formal or informal

Modern or classical

Inside or outside

Have you ever just sat in your office staring at the walls thinking and thinking - waiting for some magical inspiration?

Move! Get out of the space you are in and try a different one.

If you have to think of ideas for an outdoor product - get outside!

You may need a new perspective - try the basement or the boardroom, the roof or the garden - hop on a bus, take a train. Where you are changes how you feel and how you feel changes how you think.

You do not have to stay at your desk or go to a meeting room! Try stepping out of your four walls - don't get boxed in!

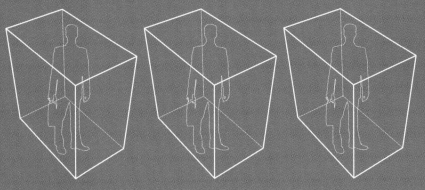

open

If you are trying 'expansive thinking'

ie. "how far can this idea go?" then you need a big space.

S p a c e

Go to the seaside and stare out to sea.
Imagine your idea filling the space.

The wide open expanse makes you
think more clearly and expansively. Feel
the movement of the waves and with
each wave try to improve on the idea.
Use the force of nature to make you
aware of the possibilities.

(I know you are thinking we have lost the
plot now but believe me it works - see
the Wrong Thumb exercise on page 128)

Open space. Wide open spaces can clear your mind.

Get into the countryside and see how far
you can see.

Stretch your ideas to the horizon.

And if anyone asks you where you are going - say proudly you are going to spend some time thinking!

wrong thumb

[Fig 1]

Put both your hands together in front of you

[Fig 2]

Intertwine your fingers and cross your thumbs as comfortably and naturally as you can

[Fig 3]

Now unwind your thumbs

[Fig 4]

And cross them in the opposite direction

How does that feel? A bit strange - just like a strange new business book or a weird new method of thinking... odd, but keep reversing your thumbs over and over, and it doesn't feel strange anymore. That's just like doing anything new... keep practicing and soon it will be normal.

There is a special sensation you feel when you are outside your comfort zone of thinking. Minds love to be in a rut - to do things the way they always have - sooo much more comfortable, sooo much easier.

Wake up your lazy mind - show it who's boss, be aware of the creative feeling. Try the 'wrong' thumb exercise.

How does that feel? **ugh!**

Now cross your thumbs over again and again until it feels normal either way. That is what thinking in new ways is like - strange at first then normal.

You just have to:

1   Be aware that your mind is lazy

2   Wake it up

3   Keep thinking new things in different ways and show it who's boss

competition fuels the fire

Humans, by their very nature, are competitive. Use this natural gift to your advantage.

Competition makes me come alive. There's nothing I like doing more than winning.

We often use this physical pressure to great effect. At work you can get different departments or different offices competing against each other to win a prize by coming up with the best ideas or solutions, or even the most.

If you want to use your competitive nature to enhance your performance you must try to understand what makes you want to be competitive. It's different for everyone... some people just want to win, other people might decide that it's because they don't want to lose! What about pride or simply the glory? You choose yours. What reward do you want?

Focus on how it would feel if you were to win or get the glory. Use that feeling to stimulate and incentivise you to put the effort in that will be necessary for you to achieve your objective.

Competition is a powerful weapon. It can focus your mind more acutely than any other method. In the last century there was a surge of scientific developments during the period of the two world wars.

There was an obvious need to achieve. How can you use that thought to help focus your mind?

Competition also gives you a benchmark for your ideas... are they as good as or better than your opponents'? It gives you a focus.

Competition can harden the issues. I asked one of our departments what words describe the effect of competition - here are some of their answers:

exacting, directing, specific, reason, hard, focused, logic

As you can see these words are definite, black and white. Competition can be described as clarifying or intensifying the thinking.

Can competition narrow your thinking? Yes it can, because it focuses your mind on the moment and some people - particularly in a commercial environment - use this narrowing of their thinking to create immediate responses.

why not just **walk** away?

It is received wisdom that you should never walk away from a problem.

However, creative thinking is one area where this rule definitely

does not apply! **Creativity should never be hard work.** In fact,

the minute you start to struggle the best thing to do is just stand

up and walk away, and I mean that literally.

Leave your desk and just take a break. Remember, you may stop

working but your brain never does.

Often the answer to your creative problem is lying there, dormant,

all it takes to release it is deliberately not thinking about it. How is

it that the answer to a problem pops into your head first thing when

you wake up?

You don't need to be a neurologist to figure out what's happened

- quite simply, you've slept on it.

coffee
cherries
ginseng
toffee
caffe latte
shellfish
coca-cola
chunky kit kats
chocolate
capuccino
marshmallow
ice-cream
tim tams
strawberries
coconut
wine

Bananas - trigger endorphins which enhance your mood

Chocolate - stimulation for the brain in the form of noradrenaline

Fun Foods - jelly beans, cola bottles, fizzy drinks, ice-cream fun food - feel good

Why not combine them and make a banana split for your next creative meeting?

Notice how some foods make you feel different - alert, happy, sleepy ...

Notice how you eat certain foods - popcorn is shovelled by the handful, handmade Swiss chocolates are treasured one by one, mints are treated more casually.

Some foods have ritual attached. How do you eat - an artichoke, an oyster, a hot dog?

Think about how your product or service is handled or consumed.

Think about what food might help you think about your next idea: something fun, something young, something serious, something luxurious, something healthy, something indulgent

Think about your mood - it is often best to be in a positive state when trying to think.

Why not try food for a boost? Some foods have an immediate effect on our performance and mood.

A natural high? Neuro-transmitters transport information around your brain

Food for thought - try these in meetings

Seratonin - the happy hormone
Nuts, Bananas, Sweets, Dates, Figs, Pineapple

Acetylcholine - keeps you alert, relaxed, optimistic
Sesame seeds, Cheese, Nuts

Dopamine - helps us to day-dream and imagine
Milk, Cheese

Noradrenaline - stimulates the brain and is an antidepressant
Apples, Nuts, Chocolate

It has been proven that certain foods can directly affect your mood. As it is true that how you feel affects how you think, it is worth experimenting with foods for thought!

Some foods can actually make you feel good and make you more energetic - both excellent states for thinking, **so consider eating some thinking foods the next time you need ideas.**

Why not combine them and make a banana split for your next creative meeting?

Research has proven a direct link between certain foods and brain function. We have been told that fish is brain food and this is true. Fish has choline which the brain uses to make acetycholine needed for communication between the neurons involved in memory and cognitive reasoning. Dramatic drops in acetycholine often go hand in hand with memory loss and other signs of Alzheimer's disease. The Japanese have the highest IQs in Asia and they eat a lot of fish!

In 1999 The Guardian reported that experiments with dieters showed that they did less well in thinking tests than the well fed.

Also reported was a study by a psychologist - David Benton, at the University of Wales, Swansea: 832 young females were asked to recall a list of words 30 minutes after breakfast and 3 hours after breakfast. They found the task significantly easier straight after breakfast - one theory is that breakfast supplied the brain with the necessary blood glucose to improve memory. **Eat breakfast!**

So eat up
for your brain's sake!!

food
for thought

The CAT SAT on THE MAT

The cat sat on the mat (by the window) the cat was looking carefully at the fish on the window ledge.

We asked 25 children aged 8-10 from Everton Primary School in Nottinghamshire to picture 'The Cat Sat on the Mat'. These are some of the results. There is creativity in diversity. Different cats, different mats and different ways of sitting - each interpretation is unique.

Find the creativity in the diversity of interpretations

The cat sat on Mat.

I'm Mat.

It is fantastic that every one of us is unique in our thinking process. Say one simple thing to a group of people and every one of them will process that information in their own creative way. This is interesting as we often make the mistake of assuming we are understood - in reality it is more probable that no one else understands what you mean at all - well, not exactly what you mean.

This can be frustrating but also an invaluable resource for creative ideas. Just try making a statement about the issue you need ideas for in a room of individuals. Then just ask them what they saw - ask what visual image they conjured up in their minds. Use the variety to spark new ideas.

"As a teacher we tend to structure an awful lot of the curriculum and the children found it hard to work on such an open task, with no direction at all."

Judith Hague Class teacher

If you want creativity, try asking a young person

Thinking

How does a.

How do our brains think of new ideas? Like new transport for instance, well, this is how I'd think of a new form of transport.... I'd take a form form of transport that is already around, like, a car. Then, I'd take something from it, away like it's wheels and add something new like Hover Jets, and then you have a new form of transport, the Hover Car! After that I'd think of start doing the same to other forms of transport, so, hover how about a hover bus?! Buses? It's simple really, our minds are like webs, we use pictures, like if I say beaches then you'll probably think of a picture like people building a sandcastle or people playing in the sea!

by Sara Cowman.

Sara seems to know her mind - do you?

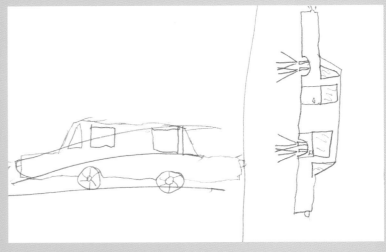

Sara Cowman **Hover car concept**

Love me hug

Think about human beings' basic needs... about what motivates and drives them. At a very basic, physical level we need water, food, warmth, shelter but on a more sophisticated, psychological level we need to feel secure, loved, admired respected... we want to be popular, we want to look good and feel good about ourselves. We want to be wealthy and healthy.

me feed me

Think about how your product or service can

Make me wealthy

Supply my basic needs

Make me look good

Make me popular

Make me feel good

Try to map out, from 0 - 100%, where your product benefits people most.
Then use those aspects to create new ideas.

Use all your
senses - try to
think which of
your senses
would be most
affected by the
thing you need
to think of.

sensual

Smell
Leather
Freshly baked bread
Freshly cut grass

Sound
The clunk of a car door
The roar of a Harley
The pop of a champagne cork

Touch
Softness of a baby's skin
A new leather coat
Crisp new notes

Taste
Rich red wine
Chocolate
Sherbet

Sight
The sun setting
A baby bear playing
Rolling green fields

soundsoundsounds

experience

Think of each of the senses in relation to something you have to think of. For example, for new ways with ice-cream:

How about ice-cream that really smells of melting chocolate? Or popcorn flavour that makes a popping sound when the spoon goes in?

smell smell smell

Every time you lick a stamp you use 1/10th of a calorie

When ketchup leaves the bottle, it travels at 25 miles per year

Venus's day is longer than its year

The world's termites

A crocodile can't stick its tongue out

It takes 40 minutes to boil an ostrich egg

outweigh the world's humans by 10:1

Eskimos use their fridges to keep their food from freezing

OOH REALLY?

Some things you learn really make you **think!** Gather amazing facts! You never know when an unusual fact will relate

to an issue you are grappling with, and if not - well, they are just fun to know and you'll be a hit at Who Wants to be a Millionaire.

A CAT HAS 32 MUSCLES IN EACH EAR

A PINT OF HIPPO MILK HAS 600 CALORIES

you may consider a nugget of
an idea quite insignificant,

from acorns

oak trees grow

but with a little thought it will crystallise into a little gem.

"I can't believe that,"

SAID ALICE

"Can't you?" the Queen said in a pitying tone. "Try again, draw a long breath and shut your eyes."

Alice laughed. "There's no use trying," she said. "One can't believe impossible things."

"I dare say you haven't had much practice," said the Queen. "When I was your age, I always did it for half an hour a day. Why, sometimes I've believed as many as six impossible things before breakfast."

Alice Through The Looking Glass

reading list and things to try

>read

Anything by Lewis Carroll

The New Scientist

Design magazines

Tony Buzan

>see

Watch the movies:

What Dreams May Come

A Beautiful Mind

Fly over the Grand Canyon in a helicopter

Shallow dive off Angel Falls

>do

Read through this book when you need ideas

Keep a record of ideas you have but don't use

Stay healthy and happy

Travel far and wide

Learn to be a ventriloquist

Something different

Laugh often

Travel everywhere you can!

Sleep with someone famous

Swim with dolphins

Travel the world

Love and be loved

Be a princess for the day

Try out your dream job

Throw caution to the wind

Always walk on the sunny side of the street

Don't worry, be happy

Have theme tunes for different moods

If you want to be original be yourself

Learn to play the piano

Do what you are most passionate about

Carpe diem

Win the lottery

Fly in a hot air balloon

Go on a blind date

Parachute jump

Spend a month's wages in the first week

Do something for charity

credits

Thank You	for
Sir Tom Farmer OBE	Contribution and Inspiration
Alan Flood	Friendship, Art & Contribution
Mary Sara	Curator & Art Critic
Claire Archibald	Friendship & Poetry
Fred Wright	Intellectual input
Cella Rowe	Energy & Intellect
Anna Harris	Thoroughness & Analysis
Mark Allin	Vision & Support
Grace Byrne	Expertise & Direction
James Davies	Writing
Sara Cowman	Visionary Thinking
Chris Arden	Art Direction
Deborah Parker	Design
Stefan Fields	Design
Stuart Hale	Design & Illustration
Bryan Wilman	Photography & Design
Ken Tiplady	Design & Illustration
Mark Culf	Project Management
Emma Hornby	Project Management
Sarah Scott	Project Management
Richard Bandler	Creating NLP
Edward de Bono	Inspirational thinking
Lewis Carroll	Writing
Argos	Client case study
Cadbury	Client case study
B. Braun	Client case study
npower	Client case study
Rachel and Peter	Providing alcohol & TLC at our local
Karen Spencer	Everything!
PKF and NatWest	Joining in our creative questionnaire testing
Tony Buzan	Mapping Minds
Sharon Hodgson	For technical preparation skills
Mat Tyrrell	For technical preparation skills
The team at outside the box	Support, ideas and inspiration